PRECISELY
THE PROPHETIC

What Else Could Possibly Go Right?

RUSSELL AND KITTY WALDEN

Dedication

This book is dedicated to Denise Allsop. Your faithfulness and friendship has buoyed our spirits and kept us encouraged as God took us from homelessness to the leadership of a global ministry touching millions. Thank you for your kindness, your devotion and your love.

Also, to Lisa Brassler, Chris and Isabel Richman, and their daughter Jenna Sophia. Your generosity helped make this book happen. Thank you.

Acknowledgments

We heartily acknowledge Ken Allen, Terri Allen, Katie Kahre and Georgette Thompson for their committed work of editing this book and making it better in the process.

TABLE OF CONTENTS

Introduction

Precisely the Prophetic is the narrative of two lives adrift in an unprecedented level of favor and divine outcomes. Kitty and I met one another later in life while working together on a kingdom assignment that would serve to bring our ministries together in 2007 and ultimately marriage and the launching of Father's Heart Ministry in 2010. During those years we were lifted from homelessness and poverty to the leadership of a ministry with a worldwide reach touching the lives of over 10 million through our online channels including the FHM website, www.fathersheartministry.net. In short, in just twelve years, we have brought the gospel in demonstration and power to multitudes of people in the US and around the world.

How did all this happen? Not by human origination. We were working in the IT sector (Russ) and the hospitality industry (Kitty) when God reached into our lives and spring boarded us into our highest heart's desire and greatest dream fulfilled.

In the beginning, Father's Heart Ministry was just an outlet for our hunger to share the gospel while we continued in the work-a-day world. Then one day, a lady in Australia sent in an e-mail. She appreciated what she had read online and wanted to know how to send us a donation. A donation? That was a new thought for us. I built websites for a living for over 20 years, therefore such things were not new to me, but we just hadn't thought of making a donation link available. The next day, just for this little lady "down under" we put a link up so she could donate. To our surprise, support started flowing in. Next, we put a link for visitors to subscribe to the FHM e-mail list. Within a very short time, there were so many subscribers we had to find a different technology to handle this new-found fruitfulness. Then the calls came for us to travel to the far-flung nations of the world to share the message of the Father's Heart. What was that message? That love never fails to produce something. It never fails to produce more love. This message emphasis resonated with the people, and the response that came back to us was utterly unanticipated. We weren't groping or flailing about, desperate for some ministry opportunity. We were inundated with invitations and requests. Suddenly our everyday life was filled with calls for us to go out to preach, teach, and prophesy.

Before we did any ministry assignments overseas, the Father interrupted our plans with a mandate for the nation. We were driving back to our home in Republic, Missouri, from a vacation time visiting Royal Gorge in Colorado. Kitty loves what she calls "windshield time" and had done most of the driving that day. As we left the eastern face of the Rockies behind, the featureless Kansas prairie stretched out before us for what seemed like endless hours. Kitty became sleepy, so I took the wheel so she could rest. After not quite an hour, she stirred, and I had something on my mind to share with her.

"SOOO," I began, "I want to tell you something I heard the Father say while you were sleeping."

Kitty nodded to indicate she was listening, and I continued to communicate to her that the Father had informed me that we were going to go to 12 major cities across the nation in the next year and the year after that we would go to 12 countries around the world. What about our home and our things? Were we to turn our business over to others while we fulfilled this assignment? Were we to put our possessions in storage or to hire someone to housesit for us while we dove into this new assignment? While we certainly knew God was speaking, these other answers weren't so clear.

Kitty contemplated all these things, and we discussed perhaps finding a storage place for our furniture and just giving up our rented home during this season of travel. We had the same things most Americans have – a couch, dining room set, living room set, etc. – and as Kitty turned this over in her mind, the Father interrupted her:

"Kitty, what do you do with a couch?"

She answered, "well, Lord, you sit on it."

The Father replied, "Is that what you want to do? You must want to sit?"

It was then that we decided to give away all we owned down to the last fork and knife. We only kept our clothes and a few essentials that were packed in the car for life on the road. What would we do for money? Well, we did have some money left over from the sale of a second car, and I thought the amount would be enough to get down the road for at least three weeks. Then the Father interrupted again.

"I want you to take the money from the sale of that vehicle and lay it at your mentor's feet (Prophet Walter Waller)."

What a challenge. We would be going out with just enough money to sustain us for maybe a week or more. We were a little thoughtful (concerned) about that, and God must have laughed because He knew the end from the beginning. This was not to be an odyssey of deprivation. What we thought would be 12 cities over the course of an entire year on the road non-stop, turned out to be 66 meetings in as many cities. During this year that we dubbed the "Jericho drive," we turned down 120 invitations while we traveled coast to coast four times in 12 months. There was no groundwork. We didn't scrounge around to find a friendly church where we could hold a meeting on our way to the next town. We trusted God, and God came through. As we preached and prophesied our way coast to coast, ministries were launched. Churches started. The word of the Lord changed lives as we met in homes, in small groups, hotel venues with very little preplanning and yes an occasional church. People began calling us "Mama Kitty and Papa Russ." The Father's Heart was manifesting as we advocated for the prophetic and prophesied and preached to several thousand over that year and in the years that followed that number grew from 1000s and then 10's of 1000s and later on multiplied millions as God showed up in a demonstration of power and miracles and glory. During that time, we formed relationships and connections with people all over the US that have endured for years. (More on the Jericho Drive in a later chapter.)

In all of this, we were moving from faith to faith and glory to glory. There was never a moment of downturn. Indeed, in the years since, every season has seen the hand of God's supply so faithfully that not once have we been forced to say "we can't obey God and go to this country or that city because there is no money…" This has been the hallmark of our lives. We have walked in breakthrough in business, in our personal lives and our ministry. We have lived in the "sweet spot" of God where according to Amos 9:13, the plowman overtakes the reaper, and the seeds of obedience produce a harvest before they hit the ground.

What does any of this have to do with you? Much in every way. Many ministers will tell of the demands of their lives and make the statement "I wouldn't wish these things on anyone - the challenges and suffering involved (they allege) as I have laid down my life to serve God would be too great for anyone to bear…" On the other hand, Kitty and I don't have any sad stories to tell. God has blessed us consistently every step of our lives for the last 12 years. Because of this unparalleled favor, we have something to communicate to you.

We want YOU to have YOUR VERSION of our life of breakthrough, benefit, and blessing.

We have something to impart, and this book is one part of our mandate to do just that. What would your breakthrough look like? Your vision might be different from ours but the promise of God is the same. Perhaps instead your dream is to move into business or to excel in sports or some other endeavor that stirs your heart. Remember this – the ache in your heart is the prophecy over your life. God never causes you to long for something that He does not fully intend to bring about – with your cooperation and yieldedness.

The things that we have experienced are not random or exclusive only to us. Neither did they come to pass as a result of some instantaneous dollop of Holy Ghost blessing that didn't require cooperation on our part. We walked day by day in obedience in these things – this life of incredible grace and fulfillment – by God's anointed process, and for that reason, we can teach YOU to experience the same thing. That is what this book is all about. Precisely the Prophetic.

2 Chron. 20:20 tells us to believe the prophets, and so shall we prosper. The original language wording there means if we believe the prophets, we will come to breakthrough, increase, and promotion. That is what we want to inspire you to. It is true that you can't get everything God gives you through a book – but beyond that end, we have an online school

(Breakthroughschool.net) and a personal face to face mentoring program that will bring our presence and testimony alongside your life that you might experience the same things. You can learn more about these things at:

www.fathersheartministry.net.

Chapter One

PRECISELY THE PROPHETIC

Russ:

When Kitty and I met, and our ministry launched, I continually told Kitty, "you are far more prophetic than I am." She found that hard to believe, but I was insistent. "Kitty I never did any of this till you came into my life…" She would simply disagree, but these are the facts. The very first time I met Kitty, she was pastoring a church in Seymour, Missouri. I was the assistant overseer of the denomination that gave her church its charter. It was my job to visit all the congregations under our care, so in that official capacity, I went to preach for Pastor Kitty. During the ministry time, I called her up, and taking her hand, God spoke:

"Kitty the Father shows me you are a ballistic missile for God. Not everyone is going to be happy about what the Father does in your life, but you just keep obeying the Father and let those people experience the woodshed of God for their judgments and criticisms…"

With that final word in the Sunday morning service, I made my exit and didn't hear from Kitty or know what became of her. Twelve years passed and I saw a newspaper clipping that she was in Branson, Missouri taking care of Hurricane Katrina victims. I called her up and found she needed some help organizing a new ministry. The Father whispered to me that I should make arrangements to help her. When I arrived in Branson, I found Kitty to be the person I remembered. She was full of the Holy Spirit and burning with a passion for Christ. From the very beginning, the Lord melded our hearts together, and in due course, we joined our ministry efforts together, and Father's Heart Ministry was launched.

Father's Heart Ministry is a team effort. Kitty and I are a power couple in the kingdom. Most of the time, when we minister, we do so in a tag team way before the people. Our emphasis is on the prophetic and the outpouring of God's Spirit through a message of love because love never fails. Love makes faith work. Without it you are useless in the kingdom. Who would want to hear a word from a prophet who didn't move in the love of God? From the very beginning, Kitty had an innate grasp and understanding of what God was doing in our lives as she shares below:

Kitty:

Where did this book's title "Precisely the Prophetic" come from? One day a former pastor of mine named Tim Snyder at Healing Rivers in Branson, MO, had made a statement in a prophecy that had caught my attention. In a Sunday morning service, he prophesied for around 20 minutes, in which, a portion of that prophetic word said that:

"The revival that is coming will have an element of Pensacola, but it won't be Pensacola, it will have an element of Toronto, but it will not be Toronto... It will have an element of each of these great moves of God," Pastor Tim concluded, "but there is an additional element to this move that is coming, and I can't tell you what it is..." That word placed a question in my heart about the coming move of the Spirit that would radically change my life.

A year later, I was on vacation driving out to California to visit some relatives. As I drove along a stretch of road in the desert, the memory of that prophetic word came up in my spirit. I recalled Pastor Tim's prophecy about the missing element in the coming outpouring of God. As the miles passed by, I got quiet before the Lord and asked the Father, "what's the element? What's the missing element that we are believing for that is going to characterize the coming outpouring of your Spirit? Instantly the Father replied back to me and said, "It is Precisely the Prophetic."

Russ:

Why would God bring a move of His Spirit with an emphasis on the prophetic? Didn't Jesus warn us about prophets coming in the last days in opposition to His kingdom? Let's look at the exact verse:

[Mat 24:11 KJV] 11 And many false prophets shall rise, and shall deceive many.

Why do you think false prophets will come? If there

11

are false prophets (and indeed there are many), then there must also be true prophets. If there is a counterfeit move of the Spirit, then there must certainly be an authentic move as well. Think about it. If you were running a cash register at the gas station and someone handed you a crisp, pristine $13 bill, would you accept it? No, you wouldn't because there are no GENUINE $13 bills printed by the US Mint. It's the same thing regarding the prophetic. The enemy brings false prophets into the earth because there are likewise many genuine, God called, authentic prophets comprising an entire move of the Spirit that we must not ignore.

What is your thinking about the prophetic? In Eph. 4:11-12, we read the following:

[Eph 4:11-12 KJV] 11 And he gave some, apostles; and some, prophets; and some, evangelists; and some, pastors and teachers; 12 For the perfecting of the saints, for the work of the ministry, for the edifying of the body of Christ:

Who is the "He" in this verse? It's talking about Jesus. Jesus came out of the grave leading captivity captive, and before He ascended up on high, He stopped long enough to impart five "office gifts" to the church, including the office of the prophet. There is no record of that office ever being withdrawn by the hand of God's providence. That means that since there are pastors and teachers and evangelists in the earth, therefore, there MUST BE prophets and apostles. Let me ask you a question. Who is your pastor? Unless you are a part of a small minority of people who don't believe in having a pastor when I asked that question the name and face of your pastor came up before you. You need to have a pastor. Pastors are not optional. Isn't that true? If you met someone in the grocery line and they professed Christ but didn't see the need for ever having a pastor, wouldn't you be concerned about that? You would remember all the sweet and tender moments when you were in great need, and your pastor was there for you.

When you look at the list of ministries in Eph. 4:11-12 is the pastor singled out as being different than the other four ministries? Is the pastor like the steering wheel of a car (every car must have one) but the prophet, for instance, is optional like a moon-roof? That is how we tend to think about the prophetic, but it is contrary to what Eph. 4:11-12 implies. If you need a pastor (and you do), then you also need a prophet. 2 Chron. 20:20 tells us that prophets are in our lives to prosper us (that word "prosper" in that verse means "come to breakthrough"). So, the question is, "who is the prophet in your life?" If you do not know, then you do not have one. That needs to change. Pastors are here to mature and nurture us. Prophets are here to bring us through their influence to a place of blessing and breakthrough that the other ministries are not intended to operate in. Pastors don't make good prophets and prophets don't make good pastors. We need both, and they are two different offices that we need in our lives along with the others mentioned in Eph. 4. Let's look at 2 Chron. 20:20:

[2Ch 20:20 KJV] Believe in the LORD your God, so shall ye be established; believe his prophets, so shall ye prosper.

Notice in the verse above that believing the Lord and believing the prophets are two different things. A dear mother who believed the prophets asked her son if he wished a prophet to pray over him. He smirked and answered, "mom – I've got Jesus, I don't need a prophet..." That is a foolish answer by a foolish young man. He was established because he believed the Lord, but he wasn't prospering, in fact, he was in his 30's still living with his mom spending all day frittering on his computer. That doesn't sound like a breakthrough to me but if he had obeyed 2 Chron. 20:20 then things would have been different for him. Someone else answered the question who was their prophet by naming a prophet who died recently. How convenient to make such a claim. A dead prophet will no doubt tell you all you want to hear with no accountability at all. What if you thought that way about your pastor? What if you told someone that brother so-and-so was your pastor, but that pastor had been in a graveyard for 20 years? That would be ridiculous. We need the prophets.

The move of God that the Father showed Kitty was described as "Precisely the Prophetic." We need to know that the prophetic is not an end in itself. John the Baptist was a prophet whose office was to bring forth Jesus the apostle and high priest of our faith (Hebrews 3:1). We see then that the prophet is intended to be a forerunner of the apostle. Most prophets don't get that, and even John struggled, and as a result, he lost his head. He didn't like how Jesus was operating and challenged him, and the next thing we know he was gone. Strangely many prophets in our day have died before their time of head wounds, brain cancers, and things related to accident and disease affecting the head. Could it be we need to reassess the prophetic move and realize it is destined not to be an end in itself but to bring forth something much greater?

The prophets operate in demonstration of the Spirit. Apostles primarily move in demonstration of power (or at least they should). This was true in John the Baptist's case as well. Read the following verse:

[John 10:41 KJV] 41 And many resorted unto him, and said, John, did no miracle: but all things that John spake of this man were true.

John the Baptist moved in demonstration of the Spirit as a prophet, but he did not move in the demonstration of power. Why is that important to make note of? John the Baptist did no miracle BUT Jesus didn't do any miracles until He was baptized of John in the Jordan. What does this tell us? It indicates to us that the demonstration of the Spirit in the Prophetic is intended by God to be the forerunner of the demonstration of power that is coming and that will be accompanied by validated, empowered apostles of God in the earth. Did you know that the early church fathers believed that just as there were 12 founding apostles of the Lamb that there would be

12 finishing apostles raised up in the second millennia from their day? We are living in that time! God has raised up the prophets to make room for outpouring of the power of God in the end time flowing through a seasoned, validated restoration of apostolic authority and power in the earth. That is why the current and emerging movement of the Spirit is "Precisely the Prophetic" to make room for the greater works that are coming in the demonstration of power!

Chapter Two

CALLED FROM MY MOTHER'S WOMB

Russ:

When I was born, I came quite early and consequently was a very tiny baby. Things in 1960 were not like they are today in terms of premature infant survivability. The 1960 mortality rate for infants was double what it is today. To complicate things, my mother Ruth Walden was significantly diminished in her health, having suffered from severe chronic respiratory problems that had left her hospitalized or in a tubercular asylum for a large portion of her childhood and young adult years. When I was born, I was so tiny I could lay in the nurse's hand with the tops of her fingers showing above my head and my ankles dangling off her palm. To increase my chance of survival, the doctors at Kansas City Memorial Hospital put me in an iron lung for the first three months of my life.

I was the third and last of the children born to my parents, and Mom was looking forward to cuddling me. However, because of the time I spent in the iron lung, she would be disappointed. When she left me in my crib alone, I would rest quietly. When she picked me up; however, I would become fussy until she laid me back down by myself. She remarked that when she picked me up, I cried, and when returning me to my crib, she would cry, her young mother's heart longing to snuggle me and pour affection upon me.

This type of severe isolation in my earliest days would have a long-term effect. Often I find that I crave solitude in the same way others desire food. I was quite shy and suffered much at the hands of bullies and school mates. I would seldom make eye contact and avoided having to stand up in front of my class at all costs with one exception. When I moved from elementary school to the seventh grade, the English teacher gave the class writing assignments. Something stirred in me as I wrote creatively for the first time. An inborn drive to write surfaced in me that did not go unnoticed by my teacher. She fanned those embers, and the coals became an veritable flame. To make room for my writing, she told me not to worry about any of the regular assignments in the class. She gave me permission and encouragement to write short stories, developing them all week and then on Friday's she would suspend the regular lesson plan to read what I wrote to the entire class.

These weekly story times were highpoints in my young life. I would use my classmates as characters in my stories, casting them in various adventures in the storylines that I would craft for their entertainment. Looking back on this time in the light of my great shyness I was surprised at how disclosing I was of my thoughts about my classmates and other aspects of my personal life that these short stories revealed about myself. The teacher met with my parents and encouraged them to seek out tutors and special programs to foster my writing ability. It was not to be. Mom and Dad loved me, but there were priorities other than my academic development, and they couldn't see their way through toward me doing anything more than the same mundane schoolwork of the rest of my classes. In time, as teenage years commenced, my passion for writing faded until much later in my adult life.

My family background was one of natural impoverishment but spiritual riches beyond measure. The Walden family was generationally disadvantaged, and Mom and Dad struggled to lift us above the poverty line and into the middle class. They owned several successful businesses, including being one of the top painting contractors in Kansas City with a very elite clientele. Opportunities for advancement and increasing the family's wealth were frequent in coming to my father. In one instance he was offered the contract for the interior of the newly constructed Waikiki Hilton, with a lifetime position in Hawaii after the job was complete. He turned it down. Being a devout full gospel believer with a call to preach, he was confident that Jesus would come back soon and that compelling fact would not allow him to pursue such worldly goals. There was a lost and dying humanity all around him, and he longed to fulfill the mantle of ministry that lay on his life.

Dad was raised by John and Opal Walden in Henry County, Missouri, during the depression years. My grandfather made his living as a bare-knuckles fist fighter and calling barn dances and square dances in the cities of Butler and Clinton, Missouri. For several generations going back to great, great, great grandfather William, who was a civil war veteran, there was no faith life in evidence in this branch of the Walden clan. Life was hard, and Dad and his siblings grew up under the rigors and burden of the Depression-era. They lived in tar paper shacks out by the railroad tracks with barely enough food to keep them going. Grandpa John was a hard man with strict ways, not looking any further than his hardened fists to beat men senseless in prizefighting for making his living. Then one day, God sent someone his way that changed all that.

Grandpa was outside the house checking on the chicken coop when a man he later described as a "pipe smoking Methodist" came into the yard looking for children to gather up for the Vacation Bible School that his church put on each summer. Grandpa wiped his hands on his faded overalls and shook hands with the man. That Methodist spoke things into John's heart that moved him deeply, and when the man asked him to accept Jesus as his savior, John began to weep profusely under the conviction of the Holy Ghost. The man stepped over and wrapped his arms around John like a loving father. He told John that Jesus loved him and that he loved him in Christ. Grandpa would later testify that up until that moment; no human being had ever said to him that he was loved. As a result, he plunged his life into the things of God and quickly identified and accepted the call to ministry.

Grandpa John's wife Opal was born again immediately after he was and they gathered up the children in the buckboard (in the 1930's mind you) and found their way to the "Old Red Barn Church." It was called the Old Red Barn Church because it met in a crude, hay-strewn abandoned red barn on the wrong side of town. Soon after they began attending, the young couple was filled with the Holy Spirit with evidence of speaking in other tongues. Dad and his three siblings as young as they were, gave their hearts to Jesus likewise, and he immediately gave proof of a call to the gospel. When company came to visit the Walden house, my Dad (at the age of seven) would gather all the children inside the woodshed at the back of the house and set out nail kegs and a makeshift pulpit where he would preach a salvation message to his young cousins and playmates. The adults would sneak over and look in the windows at these children playing at church. It was more than play however, as Dad recalled years later that there were children whose families had no spiritual light in them whatsoever who gave their lives to Christ in that woodshed and carried a lifelong testimony of faith from that time forward.

This was the background that I was born into in August of 1960 in Kansas City. During those years what became known as the Latter Rain Revival from the 1940s was still going strong 20 years later. Mom and Dad were immersed in this outpouring and in the Healing Revivals that raged during those days. They attended meetings with William Branham, AA Allen, Jack Coe, Oral Roberts, and others. When the tent preaching season would close for the year, Dad would hire out of work tent preachers to work in his painting business. After hours these preachers would all go to mom and Dad's house spending hours in prayer and seeking God's face for greater glory and outpouring. I was only in diapers at this time, and I would waddle in among these spiritual giants and my Dad, taking a place of prayer kneeling at a big overstuffed chair.

Before I was born, a prophet visited the house for dinner. As my very pregnant mom-to-be cleared the dishes away the man took on a distant look in his eye and commenced to prophesy to my parents that this child yet to be born would be filled with the Holy Ghost in his mother's womb. In that moment like Elizabeth of old when she carried John the Baptist – I leaped in my mother's womb with a great show of activity. Mom and Dad took this as confirmation of the words of the prophet. Fast forward to the time as a toddler praying with the preachers and prophets in my parent's living room. Dad spied me kneeling in prayer and could faintly hear my little voice raised to God as the others who were praying as well. Dad came to my side to listen more clearly, and just as the prophet said, he found me praying in a distinct and clear prayer language by the word of the Lord. In this, they sensed that all the warfare and My near death as an infant that God had something in mind for me and that there was a calling upon me for exploits in the kingdom of God.

What is the lesson to take away from this for your life? Never rule out the dealings of God with young children. When as a young child, my Dad prayed and preached in the woodshed with his playmates – he wasn't taken seriously by the parents looking on. They thought they were just playing church, and that was all there was to it. What they should have noticed was the genuine emotion in these children's faces as Dad preached. They might have paid particular attention to those little ones slain in the spirit before the Lord at that makeshift altar doing business with God in their hearts. These things gave Mom and Dad particular sensitivity when they witnessed similar situations in My young life even as a toddler.

Years later, at the age of seven, I gave my life to Jesus and was born again. At the time the family had moved from Kansas City to their home town of Clinton Missouri They were returning from church meetings in Lawrence, Kansas. We were listening to AA Allen preach on the radio as the miles whizzed by on old Highway 13. As they were passing through Peculiar Missouri, Allen declared over the radio "Folks! The Lord killeth and maketh alive – God's in a killin' mood tonight!" Something about that touched my young heart, and from the back seat, I tugged on my daddy's sleeve asking, "that's not true, is it daddy?" Immediately Dad turned to the side of the road, and right there in Peculiar Missouri, my parents prayed

Me through to the assurance of my salvation.

Chapter Three

BANKING WITH JESUS

Kitty:

I was born to a family with five girls (including myself) and one boy. From the very beginning, the enemy made a play for my life, but God was there with me even in the womb. When my mom went into labor with me at an air force base hospital in Merced, CA, the doctors said, Mrs. Hawkins, I feel skull bones here, when he had examined her. She said, "You don't say that to a lady who is in labor and is about to give birth." He said, "Mrs. Hawkins, you have twins. There are two babies, but one doesn't have a heartbeat." So, they discovered that my twin sister died at about seven months in the womb because she had no liver, and other major organs were not functioning. So, they took that baby. I was about 6 lbs. 4 oz. and mom said they had to watch me really close because they didn't know if that stillborn baby would have affected my health.

Years later, as an adult, I was in a room with 250 people when Prophet Bill Lackie at Christian International called me out. He said, "Lady, there is a spirit of death on you, but it's not anything you did, it was something that was done to you, and it has been tracking you all your life." When I went to prayer about it much later, the Father said that it was the baby that had died in the womb. So, that death spirit was still trying to take me out. The enemy was trying to make that happen several times growing up, but it never happened because nobody is bigger than my Father God.

Let me tell you about my salvation experience. When I was growing up, I was exposed to the church. Early on, Mom had us in a Methodist Church. My dad had mostly been raised Seventh Day Adventist and then Baptist. It was exciting because I was so thrilled to get to go to the revival meetings they were having at the Methodist tent they had in Brownsmills, NJ. I remember when I was nine years old, I was sitting in the back with my sisters, and I believe the Sunday school teacher had brought us to this evening service for the revival, and I just felt the conviction as the minister was preaching about being born again and not perishing and going to hell. I received the message of Jesus, and it just exploded on the inside of me. I wanted that. Even as a young girl, I knew I needed redemption. I wanted Jesus as my Savior. When the invitation came, I stepped out of the crowd, from the seating area and went down the aisle to the altar. I felt something brush up against me, and it was my sister Kathy who was one year and one day my senior. She kneeled there beside me to pray as well. I then gave my heart to Christ at that moment. I remember crying on that altar; my tears were on that altar because I just wanted Jesus to come into my heart.

When I stood up after they prayed with us, and we were walking back to our seats, I said, "Kathy, why did you go down to the altar?" She said, "Well, I sure didn't want to go to hell." We had a sweet laugh over that. Later she prayed, "God, I would be a missionary for you if you don't make me go to Africa." That's what she would say, growing up as a little kid.

From the very beginning, I was passionate and excited about Jesus. My family moved a lot because my dad was Air Force. I always tell people, "I was not an air force brat, I was an air force darling." That's my confession; I have stuck with it all these years. When I was in grade school, first or second grade, I remember swinging on a swing, in a city park, that was by our house, and I would swing as high as I could, and as loud as I could sing, "for God so loved the world that He gave His only son" that beautiful song, hoping, just hoping that somebody would get born again and accept Jesus as their Savior. So that was my early experience as a born-again believer. God had put in my heart from the beginning, the heart of an evangelist.

As a young teenager, we lived in Reseda, CA, which later, I came back to when I graduated from Reseda High in San Fernando Valley, CA. I remember just being so in love with my Bible at that time. Mom had transitioned us from the Methodist church to a Baptist congregation that was closer by. She would take all six of us to Sunday school at the Baptist Church in the Reseda area, and we fell in love with it. During that time, I got lots and lots of teaching and training, and even helped in the nursery; I was always volunteering in the nursery as a young teenage girl because I just love babies.

My love for the word and studying the scripture showed up strongly in that season. My mom told me one morning, "it's so sweet, I found you with your Bible laid open, on your belly, and you were sound asleep." She continued, "So I just came in and turned out the light and closed up your Bible for you." Not only did I love the scriptures, but the move of the Spirit of God was surfacing in my heart at the same time. Lying awake at night just talking to God all of a sudden, I was talking in the French language. I had never taken French, ever. However, this wasn't a child's rambling but an early experience of speaking in other tongues. Later on, I found that the Baptist church I was part of taught this was not of God but of the devil. I hadn't even considered that. I just had an experience before I knew anything and had to make a decision whether to accept what my church taught against or to go on with God and see where that took me.

When I was 18, I was able to leave home and move to Ventura, CA, where I became a banker. I had other jobs before that, like working at the Foster Freeze (which is like a Sonic) that was located across from my high school. Even earlier than this, I gained my first business experience as a young girl in school. During that time, we had learned business skills from my dad's convenience store. In later years I was grateful for this, but at the time, it seemed like slave labor. One day I had a brilliant idea, I thought, "you know, I could buy these little cinnamon suckers for a nickel apiece, and I could sell them for a dime, at school." I didn't ask anybody, I just went and spent the money that I had from babysitting and such, and I bought a sack of those lollipops. I mentioned it in my classes, and people bought them like crazy because they weren't getting candy machines in schools back then. I was just thrilled about making money.

The day came that a teacher mentioned to the principal that I was selling candy at school. I had graduated from the little suckers and was selling licorice and other candies because it was profitable. The teacher said, "you have an appointment with the principal; he wants to talk to you." I thought, "whatever for?" I didn't do anything wrong, so I wasn't afraid. I went to the principal's office. He said, "You are selling candy at school?" I said, "yes, my dad has a store in Isla Vista, and we work for him, and I get to buy whatever I want, so I was selling candy for double the money, and it's only a dime." He said, "you just cannot do that, Kitty, you cannot sell any products in this school system." I said, "well, ok," and I stopped. I was completely flabbergasted because I didn't know what could possibly be wrong. I sold to people all the time at the store. So that was my first entrepreneurial experience in early junior high.

When I was 17, I had graduated in early January from my senior class, rather than waiting until school ended in June. My dad had moved so much in his work, that my grades were such that I had many credits. The counselors said, "Kitty, you don't even have to do the second half of your senior year, with all these points you have on our grading system. In fact, for this semester, (which was the first part of my senior year), I was allowed to have four home economic classes of my choosing because I enjoy those kinds of things, cooking, baby care, etc. I just needed one English class and could graduate." That was fine with me. I was still 17, and I turned 18 in February. My dad had told all of us kids, if you want to leave home, you have to have a little money in your pocket, and you have to turn 18. That happened for me, and I moved to Ventura, CA.

As I turned 18, I became a banker because somebody in our little Baptist Church, (I was still Missionary Baptist), was the operations officer for Crocker Bank at that time. She said, "I would like to hire you because you are so outgoing, and I want to teach you to be a teller." I said, "I would love to have a full-time job to support myself," and so I took on banking as a career. About the second or third year in, and from the very beginning of my banking career, I would not withhold the truth about Jesus to anybody because His Spirit was like a water fountain down in my heart, always produces water. What was in me was a heart for evangelism; therefore, I was forever sharing Jesus because it brought me joy, and I knew it brought the Father joy.

Being in a banking environment, being the evangelist that I was, once in a while, I would get chewed out for having a little scripture calendar on my desk or something spiritual. I probably worked for three different banks in ten years, and the opposition was constant. I would get chewed out for having scripture references on little plaques, etc., on my desk. The supervisor would come up behind me and say, "You get that off your desk." I would say, "it's just about Jesus." I didn't take it off my desk, because she couldn't make me take it off my desk. What I noticed was people being resentful about God being who He is, and Jesus as our Savior and I didn't know about the Holy Spirit working with me much, but I knew who He was later.

Even in the face of persecution, I was promoted continuously in the bank. I went from head teller to assistant operations officer, and later, I was offered full operations officer in my career. Through it all, I continued sharing Christ and winning souls to Jesus. I would have experiences with people because I was just bubbling about Jesus and they would say, "why are you so happy?" and I would be happy to tell them. Now I'm going to show a little secret about banks. They store their extra money in the vaults, in something like safe deposit boxes. At the end of the day, as the operations officer, I would have to pull out everyone and count the bundles of money. Another teller and I were sitting, (you always had to do it in twos); on the carpeted floor inside the vault and (the bank doors were locked at this point) we were counting down all the currency. As we were sitting there surrounded by 3 or 4 million dollars this young woman with me blurts out, "Kitty, how can you know if you are living for the good guys or the bad guys?" I opened my mouth and for 15 minutes shared the plan of salvation and who the enemy was, the thief coming to kill, steal and destroy, and Jesus came that we might have life and that more abundantly, she was then in tears and accepted Jesus Christ as her Savior.

I had many moments like that in odd situations, but it was always God in the midst, giving opportunity for me to boldly give my testimony for Christ. What I noticed was it bothered me being in a public arena like that and some people didn't want to hear about God, and other people would hear it as an overflow of me talking and witnessing to somebody, and they would tell the supervisor, and say please, stop all that (blah blah blah). I was telling my family one night (because I was then married, and had two little kids) at a certain point, I said, one of these days, you guys, I'm going to have my own business, I don't know what it is, but I'm going to have my own business, and I'm going to get to share Jesus, and nobody is going to stop me. The day came that this happened which I will continue with in another chapter.

While I was a banker, about five years in, we could take extra banking classes to learn more skills and so I was allowed to go to Los Angeles, about an hour from my home in Ventura. I would drive to LA, spend the night and go to a seminar that evening and all the next day and then drive back home. The first one I went to was on Thursday morning, and it was about public speaking. The attendees would listen to someone teach you how to do very polished public speaking. I had never had anything like that, so the lady gets up and is instructing about 200-250 women. I'm about three-quarters of the way back. I'm in my early 20s and just in love with Jesus and ready for what God had next in my life. I'm learning and wanting to be teachable always, and the instructor shares with us how to do public speaking. "You start your conversation, and I'm going to show you a one-minute example, I'm going to start my conversation on the right side of the room and as I am speaking to the public I would move my head gently, gradually, across the crowd, all the way to the left side." The instructor continues, calling for at least ten volunteers and give us an example of your pubic speaking.

My hand went straight up in the air, I didn't plan it, it just went straight up in the air, and I hear this in my spirit, "tell them about Noah's ark..." It was the Father speaking. "You know about Noah's ark, tell them..." My turn came, and I opened my mouth, and I did precisely what the lady (and the Spirit of God) instructed. I started talking about Noah and how he was found faithful in the eyes of the Lord, and this happened, and the flood came, and his sons were saved, their wives and his wife, and by the time I got my head to the left side of the room, it was time. And she said, "I have to tell you, in all my experience, I have never seen a first-timer do that well. You knocked it out of the park, so to speak". Walking back to my seat, a lady calls out from the crowd, "Hey, I want to hear the rest of the story." I immediately said, "Meet me out in the hall after the meeting." Then everybody laughed. That was my first sermon, and it was only 60 seconds.

I was still attending a Missionary Baptist Church in Ventura, but I knew, something inside me was stirring, and I know it is the Holy Spirit now, told me there was so much more than what I had been experiencing. I just had a hunger and a thirst; I absolutely was emaciated wanting to know more about God. I attended church three times a week back then, twice on Sunday and once on Wednesday night and I loved it, but I still had this empty place that I wanted to be filled. It wouldn't be long before the Father would send His Holy Spirit crashing into My life, bringing about change and transformation far beyond my wildest expectations.

Chapter Four

HEARING THE AUDIBLE VOICE OF GOD

Russs:

People often ask me how I came to be a prophet, or when did I know I was a prophet? Part of the answer rests on my background and exposure to various moves of God throughout my lifetime. As stated earlier, a prophet spoke over my mother that I would be filled with the Holy Spirit from my mother's womb. Think about that. How many figures in the scripture were told similar things, and what was their role in the things of God? When Mary traveled to visit with her aunt who was pregnant with John the Baptist, there was a response from the unborn baby recorded in the Bible record:

[Luck 1:41 KJV] 41 And it came to pass, that, when Elisabeth heard the salutation of Mary, the babe leaped in her womb; and Elisabeth was filled with the Holy Ghost:

When the angel announced John's birth to his father Zechariah he was told that John, as a prophet, would be filled with the Holy Ghost while yet in Elisabeth's womb:

[Luck 1:13-15 KJV] 13 But the angel said unto him, Fear not, Zacharias: for thy prayer is heard; and thy wife Elisabeth shall bear thee a son, and thou shalt call his name John. 14 And thou shalt have joy and gladness, and many shall rejoice at his birth. 15 For he shall be great in the sight of the Lord, and shall drink neither wine nor strong drink; and he shall be filled with the Holy Ghost, even from his mother's womb.

This is a promise and an experience unique to the prophetic and not only in the instance of John the Baptist. Jeremiah had a similar thing take place but was not informed about it by any human source. It was years later when the call of God came to him that the Father filled him in on the origin of his call and the beginnings of his ministry:

[Jer 1:4-5 KJV] 4 Then the word of the LORD came unto me, saying, 5 Before I formed thee in the belly I knew thee; and before thou camest forth out of the womb I sanctified thee, [and] I ordained thee a prophet unto the nations.

Consider the implications of this. As Evangelicals, we are taught first of all that there are no more prophets. Secondly, if there were a prophet to be called out by God, he would first have to be born again according to an Evangelical soteriological formula. If you haven't been born again and signed a decision card indicating a declaration of Jesus as your savior – the church today says no way could you go on then and be baptized in the Holy Ghost or called to ministry in any way – BUT – that was exactly how things went where John and Jeremiah were concerned. Always remember that God does not align His dealings regarding men's hearts with the theological requirements of men. God is a sovereign God, and that means He can do anything He wants any time He wants, and He doesn't have to check with anyone.

When Prophet William Branham was quite young – ten years of age – he heard the voice of God in the wind of an old oak tree under which he was playing. Even in his birth, his family reported a heavenly light that shone over his crib in the one-room cabin that he was born in. There came a time in Branham's life that an angel came to him in a time of crises and remained with him the rest of his days – a source by God's power through which mighty signs, miracles, and wonders took place. My parents were exposed to William Branham's ministry along with a litany of many men and women who moved in the power of God and the power of the prophetic in the 40's Latter Rain Revival, the 50's Healing Revival and the Charismatic Renewal of the 1960s. For a prophet to prophesy over me that I would be filled with the spirit in the womb was no strange thing to Mom and Dad, they simply took it as a portent of things to come.

How did these things impact my life? For the first thing, the enemy did his best to take me out of the earth as a sickly premature baby. My birth weight was minuscule, and even today, babies that premature often do not survive. The hand of God was on me, and I grew into my preadolescent years alongside my two brothers during a time that Mom and Dad attended veritably non-stop meetings night after night in the height of the Latter Rain outpouring in the early 60s. As a very young boy, I saw many things that ingrained my young heart and mind with the reality of a speaking God who commanded miracles, raised the dead and cast out devils.

The first miracle I experienced as a young boy was resurrection from the dead. When I was about six years of age Mom and Dad were living in Miriam, Kansas which was a suburb of the Kansas City area nestled close to Grandview and Overland Park. My oldest brother was in the final years of elementary school and ran track with the other young athletes at the school. One day the track team was running laps on the field, and they inadvertently ran over a young mother rabbit and her babies. All were killed when they were trodden under except for one baby rabbit who was clinging to life. My brother, Roy Jr., took off his track shoe and put the dying rabbit inside it and took him home. When he arrived, the family was bustling around getting ready for a church service that night. An extended revival was taking place, and the family had been in church every night with no end in sight. Dad met my brother as he came in the door with the wounded creature. All of us boys, along with Mom, gathered around as Dad put the bunny in a shoebox and examined him for signs of life. It seems as though the little creature was almost gone. At the children's insistence, Dad put a light bulb on a desk lamp close to the bunny to keep him warm, and the family hurried off to service at the Latter Rain church.

Hours later, they returned home, and we rushed in to check on the bunny. He was cold and stiff. Dad felt of the little figure and detected rigor mortis had already set in. Before anyone could say a word the boys in unison spoke up:

"Pray for him, Daddy! Pray for him like the preacher says and raise him back to life!"

Dad looked down at his anxious little boys and breathed a prayer. "God if you ever wanted an opportunity to impress three little boys with your miracle-working power, here is your chance."

Then Dad prayed and commanded life back into that little bunny. To our amazement and total rejoicing when Dad put the rabbit down after praying for it – it sat up with its whiskers quivering as though it was looking for some clover to eat. The rejoicing was profound. From a clearly dead animal, a miracle had happened to make an indelible impression on my brothers and me. To commemorate the event, we named the bunny Hezekiah like the king whom God gave 15 additional years of life. The rabbit lived and thrived until it was released into the woods a few months later.

When I was eleven years old, I began hearing the audible voice of God on a regular basis. I would be playing in the yard or doing homework, and a voice that seemed to come from all around me would speak up and tell me things that were about to happen. In one instance, the voice said: "go outside and stand in the drive – your mother will be home in 10 seconds."

I went out to the drive, and counting to ten greeted mom as she came around the corner into our driveway. This was a regular and ongoing experience for over three years.

When I was just turning 13, the voice of God was speaking to me as strong as ever when a fateful encounter took place. Going through the transition to teenage years, I was struggling in my faith, and one day I told the Lord that I was "going away now" and didn't want to hear His voice any longer. The Lord replied, "you will regret that decision, but Russ, I will be here when you get back..." That began a long period of time that I descended into captivity, darkness, and drug addiction. There did come a time in my nineteenth year that I rededicated my life to the Lord, but the voice of God didn't return as it had before. Time passed, and the day came that I was ordained into the ministry with a very close older friend laying hands on me in the ordination service. At that moment, the voice of God returned, and from that time on sounded not audibly but inwardly in my life. Ultimately at the age of 45, the prophetic mantle was activated on me, and life took a radical turn into seeking the kingdom, teaching preaching and prophesying around the world.

What About You? When Father's Heart Ministry launched the Lord tasked us not only to bring the voice of God to the people but also to teach the people to hear God's voice for themselves. The Father told us, "the prophet who brings the voice of God to the people but doesn't teach them how to hear God's voice for themselves – is doing them a great disservice." Toward that end, we soon launched the online prophetic school, and as of this writing, over 4000 people have taken these courses and been activated in the voice of God and in the prophetic as well.

Chapter Five

KICKED INTO THE KINGDOM

Kitty:

During my years as a banker in California, my hunger for more of God intensified and grew stronger every day. By God's grace, there was an answer to my heart's cry living nearby. My neighbor across the street from me was an on-fire Baptist lady, and she was about 20 years my senior. Her name was Peggy Toler. We became friends, and I fell in love with her passion for God. She was so outgoing and bubbly every day we spent time together. We chatted often, and I saw how her beautiful blue eyes would just dance. Peggy was filled with joy and zeal. I sat with her in her living room one morning, and asked her, "Peggy, I'm a Baptist, and you're a Baptist, but there's just something about you that is so on fire for God, and I want that." She said, "Well, honey, honey, it's the Holy Spirit." She was the first Charismatic Christian I had ever met. It was the Holy Spirit, she explained. I said, "Well, give Him to me." Just like that, so innocent. She said, "Oh, darlin', you have a Bible." I said, "Yes, Ma'am." She instructed me, "You go back across the street, and you read your Bible. See what it says about the Holy

Spirit."

I thought, ok, but I would rather she just give me a shot of the Holy Spirit, but I didn't understand how those things worked. I raced home and began my pursuit of Bible study regarding the Holy Spirit. I went back to Peggy's house and said, "I see it now. I think they lied to me. I think they lied to me about the Holy Spirit not being for today." Peggy replied, "Yes, that's true but honey, just forgive them"

I shot back, "But Peggy, they told me tongues were of the devil." She said, "Well they're just not informed, they haven't been taught. If they don't want to learn, that is up to them, but I can see you're hungry. Whenever you would like, if you would like, I will take you to one of my Bible Studies we have once a week." In this meeting, the people would gather in a circle to study the Word, and if anybody had a prayer request, at the end they would get the chair and have you sit in the middle, and they would pray for you (in my case) to be filled with the Holy Spirit.

Peggy explained all that and said, "If you want to be filled, then why don't you come with me?" I got permission from my husband to go, and I absolutely felt God in that room when I walked in with all those people. All their eyes were sparkling. At the end of the service, the teacher said, does anybody want prayer for anything? I thought, "I want the Holy Spirit!" I shot my hand up, and the leader invited me to the chair in the front for people to be prayed for. He said a couple of preliminary things, and then I repeated my request, "I want to be filled with the Holy Spirit like Peggy." He put his hand on my head and said, "now open your mouth and praise the Lord, and I said praise the Lord, now say Hallelujah, I said Hallelujah, and then the torrent came: "shandala rhondala cotasbeshodapa! I spoke in tongues for the next two minutes, and they just let me. Flowing like a fountain, it came out of my belly. It was that river of the Holy Spirit that I had been withheld from.

The leader said, "Little sister, you have had that bottled up in there a long, long time." It made me smile because I was learning about the Holy Spirit. I went from that place to being more on fire, more evangelistic, more hungry, and I couldn't get enough of Him. I told my then spouse about what happened. I didn't really need to tell him; he saw something had shifted in me and I was on fire. I have never been "off-fire" from that moment to this day, and I am 66 years old this year.

Soon after I heard about another group of women, they were called Women's Aglow. Peggy Toler asked me if I would like to go and visit that meeting as well. I said absolutely, of course. It was during a season that I was doing daycare in my home. What happened to get to that point was this:

We had bought a house in Camarillo, CA, Ventura County and the day came that I left banking and I was able to stay home with my children. How did I go from being a banker to a stay at home mom? One day the branch manager called me over to his desk and said, "Kitty, we'd like to promote you to operations officer, because you are very skilled and good at what you do." For years I had been a teller, and I was never out of balance more than a penny, because I love "getting it right." That was before computers, and everything was done on a ledger back then, handwritten. I started as a proof operator, that's the person that runs this big machine, and you process all the checks and deposits of the day.

My boss repeated, "we would like to promote you to operations officer." I had already been a teller and teller supervisor. I had also worked as an assistant operations manager, and I said well, "Can I think about it overnight?"

"Of course," he replied. I had a great rapport with management, always did, except the ones who didn't know God and they were kind of rough around the edges, but that's ok. Later this one supervisor who wanted me to rip the scripture off of my desk got born again, filled with the Holy Ghost and spoke in tongues. Not with my help, I just sowed a seed.

After receiving the offer to be promoted, I'm driving home that night, and I hear the Holy Spirit, and I could hear a lot better because I had been filled with Him. He said, "If you'll quit your job and go home, I'll promote you." I thought, where did that come from? That didn't make any sense to me at that time, being young in the Spirit. I asked, "What did you just say, Holy Spirit?"

"If you'll go home and turn down that promotion, I will promote you." I said, "Ok." I had a lump in my throat; I was teary driving down the road just minutes to the house. I told my husband when I got to the house, and he wasn't very thrilled about it because he liked me having a full-time income. But I insisted, "I am going to obey God." He knew something had shifted because something had changed. So, I said yes to God and thanked the banker for the offer, and gave my two weeks' notice. I didn't know how I was going to be able to provide what we needed for the household, but I was thrilled that I was going to get to stay home with my children. I couldn't put two and two together on how it was going to happen, I just obeyed God first and quit my job.

About 2-3 weeks later, I needed some extra money in the budget because I was going to buy some groceries and there wasn't enough money to get all the groceries I needed. I went to my bedroom, knelt by my bed to pray. I said, "Father, you told me to quit my job, but I've got to have some groceries." I had no more finished saying that prayer when the doorbell rings out front (I had a big four-bedroom house on a corner lot). I hear the doorbell, opened the door, and it's two of our best friends from the Baptist Church. They are loaded up with bags and bags of groceries. They said, "God told us to bring you these groceries." I'm just crying, and I told them about my prayer. The Holy Spirit broke me in so sweetly and so immediately to the things of the Spirit. I could never deny that He is real.

After I got filled with the Spirit and attended that Women's Aglow meeting, I had the pastor call from the Missionary Baptist Church. I had attended several meetings and was so excited. One of my banker friends told my sister-in-law that she saw me in this Women's Aglow gathering. The banker was a good friend of my sister-in-law. My sister-in-law called the pastor and reported that I was seen at a Women's Aglow Conference with my hands raised to heaven, speaking in another tongue. She tells my Missionary Baptist pastor, and he calls me and said he would like to come with a brother so and so the deacon and would like to sit down with you and talk with you and my former spouse. I said, "Sure, come on over." I didn't know what it was about and I was so hospitable back then and even now.

The pastor (a former Pentecostal, mind you) and the deacon came over to the house and sat down at the dining room table. He said, "Sister Kitty, you are in heresy according to the Missionary Baptist doctrine. You were seen with your hands raised in a Women's Aglow meeting, and you were speaking with other tongues. Tongues are of the devil, and you cannot believe that heresy and be part of the Missionary Baptist church. I said, "Well, it's too late, I'm already filled with the Spirit. It's too late, I read my own Bible, and I saw where Jesus is the same yesterday, today and forever, and I received the Baptism of the Holy Spirit, and I feel like I've had a shower on the inside of me and I'm not about to give that up."

They said, "Well, then we will have to exclude you."

I said, "I will say it again, I believe that God can do anything He wants any time He wants. He doesn't have to check in with anybody." They were astonished that I spoke so boldly, but I had the confidence of the Holy Ghost on the inside of me. My former spouse was very shy and didn't want to say anything about it, so he was listening as he was not a confronter and didn't have the Baptism of the Holy Spirit at that time. The pastor continued, "We will have to exclude you if you won't relent and say that you were wrong. I said, "Well, I will not deny my Father, and I don't deny Jesus or the Holy Spirit.

I went on to ask about my spouse who hadn't received the Holy Spirit yet: "You can exclude me if you want to, but what about my spouse." They said, "He can still be a member because he was not seen in that position, and you can visit occasionally." I said, "Ok," I was happy that he wouldn't have to lose his place as a member of their church. The very next service was Wednesday night. I was the treasurer for the church because I was a banker and they liked that because I was honest. I took the treasury books back. I was also teaching a Sunday school class because I love children. I took back the materials for the Sunday school, and I was going to turn them in and expected to have our normal service, right? We arrived at service, greeted our friends, and sat down. The pastor gets up and announces, "Before we begin our service tonight, we have some business to take care of. Sister Kitty is found to be in heresy according to the Missionary Baptist doctrine because she believes in the speaking in tongues, miracles, signs, and wonders.

I want to entertain a motion at this time to exclude Kitty and her family from our congregation." I was shocked by all that and sat there listening. The pastor ordered us to stand up, with our two little kids 5 and 7. The motion was made and a second followed and then everybody in the church, raised their hands to throw us out except for one little senior grandma. She didn't vote against us because we were her ride. We would pick her up every single service and bring her with us on this 40-minute drive to church and back home. We loved this little lady, and she couldn't drive. She looked at us; we looked at her, and we said, let's go kids. Our elderly friend had no choice but to go with us because we were her ride. We were walking out the church doors and my daughter Jennifer, who is in heaven now, said, "Mama, why did they kick us out of their church?" I said, "It's because they think it's their church, they don't' know it belongs to Jesus, but it'll be ok."

Right after this unpleasantness, I met this wonderful group of people at a Charismatic lunch meeting that met every Thursday just up the street from my bank, where I had previously worked in Thousand Oaks, CA. I would go on Thursday, and from the very beginning, those people loved me with an everlasting love. I told them what happened; I got kicked out of the Baptist Church because I believed in speaking in tongues, signs and wonders, and miracles. The leader said, "Kitty, they didn't kick you out, they kicked you into the Kingdom and all of its fullness. I prophesy this to you that they that hunger and thirst after righteousness shall be filled. You've been hungry, you've been thirsty, the Lord says, you have been filled, and you will continue to be filled from this day on".

The next thing that happened was this pastor who was leading the luncheon every Thursday had an event. He had a prophet friend, Ray Brooks, an elderly gentleman that Tom Brock submitted to. Tom was having a home meeting with about 25 people, (if that many) and he said, "we have just started this home meeting, and it's growing pretty fast. Would you like to come?" I said yes and brought my former spouse and the kids into this on-fire situation. They were doing what the Bible said you could do, and I was so encouraged. The name of the group was called Shepard Christian Center; they named it that because in no time at all, (I'm talking weeks) that ministry exploded and couldn't even be done in a house, which was one of the member's house up in the hills in Camarillo.

Pastor Tom and Suzie Brock soon rented a warehouse in Ventura and converted it for a sanctuary. My family and I were with them in the foundation of this vibrant, exciting new church plant. They had 300 in capacity in just a little over a year, and it was still growing. At some point during that time, Pastor Tom asked if I would help him out and be supervising the teachers of all these kids that are just now coming into the church because he knew I did daycare. I said I would be glad to. I ended up ministering to 14 teachers every week and then overseeing 250 children before I was finished in that assignment. About that time, when I was busy doing that, Pastor Tom asked me to come to his office and said, "Kitty, I'd like to pay you" (he knew I had done daycare and had helped to raise these babies) "I'd like to pay you to come to the office Monday through Friday as a receptionist."

I appreciated the job offer but replied, "Tom, I don't type a lick, and I'm not interested in taking a job that involves typing." He said, "I'm not hiring you for typing skills, I want you to speak to the people, everybody that comes into the office, I want you to put them at ease, get their questions, give them some answers, you already have a lot of the answers, and they won't need to see the staff pastors. I would like for you to take that on." I ended up ministering to the people that would come in for counseling (there were lots that would come in back then). I would minister them and do very few things associated with a receptionist job; answer the phones, set up the calendar, and pray for the people.

I was learning to prophesy, and I did not know all of those years that I was praying prophetically as I had no clue what that was, I really didn't. I would tell them, and it would just come up out of my spirit, and God would target something, and people would say, how did you know that? I said, "I don't know anything, I don't even know what I know, I just know the Holy Spirit had me pray it like that."

That's all I could say. Nobody was talking about how to prophesy; they weren't teaching it; they were just doing it from the pulpit. In spite of a lack of training the free flow of the Holy Spirit was coursing through my life and with Pastor Tom's cooperation, I found myself moving deeper and deeper into the reality of the prophetic.

Chapter Six

SIGNS, MIRACLES, WONDERS, AND VISITATION

Russi:

The first miracle I experienced as a young boy at the time, was a resurrection from the dead. My elder brother brought home a dying baby rabbit on a church night. Dad put a desk lamp on the creature to keep it warm, and we hurried off to service. Upon our return, the thing had died, and rigor had already set in. While three wide-eyed little boys looked on, Dad laid hands on it, and miraculously it came to life. We named it Hezekiah because the Lord gave him a new lease on life. I was only about six at the time, but the impact this made on me was profound. We had heard all the stories in Sunday School and certainly absorbed the thunderous preaching of many Latter Rain ministers (no children's church in those days), and now we had experienced the reality of God's power at work in the earth to heal the sick, cast out devils and raise the dead.

You can't ever underestimate the impact of spiritual realities on very young children. I think we do a grave disservice to our children when we excuse them from the service as though what takes place in the adult church is of no interest to them. Is there any wonder that when they grow up they often just opt out of church altogether? When I was pastoring my second church back in the '80s, our congregation made a commitment. We declared as one that God's presence was our priority. That meant that anything, any program of our church that did not directly defer to and open us up to God's presence would be set aside. One of the programs we did away with was the children's church and nursery. God was moving in our midst, and we wanted our children by our sides to experience what the Holy Spirit was bringing about. It was a decision that paid off in young people who grew up under the move of God going on to become dedicated believers. It isn't necessary to dumb down the message of the gospel, so it is palatable to young minds. Children who are pandered to in this way grow up to be dense and unteachable adults. On the other hand, when you expose children to anointed teaching and preaching and the signs and wonders that go with them the dividends for the church and those children as they grow to adulthood will be immense.

In the late '70s, I mustered into the air force and left my parents and my home for the first time. I wasn't living for the Lord, then in fact, far from it. After walking away from the voice of the Lord at the tender age of 12, I became immersed in the dark underworld of drugs and the counter culture of the '70s. Moving into my late teens, I began dealing drugs and developed a heavy addiction to methamphetamine and illicitly obtained prescription narcotics. When I entered the air force, my duty station was in Spokane, Washington. I saw this as my chance to really make it as a drug dealer, and I got involved with a drug ring that was smuggling drugs into the country. I became so hardened during that time that even hard-core drug dealers would blush at my foul mouth and ungodly ways. More than once in a drugged stupor, I recalled waking up the next morning, realizing that I'd had a gun shoved in my face the night before. Only my parent's prayers kept me alive during that time.

While I was stationed in Spokane, I was billeted in the single man's barracks with a room all by myself. This was because no one wanted to sleep in the same room with a drug fiend filled with darkness and sin. I would turn all the lights out to make the room completely dark and then turn up my records of Satanic music as loud as I could. It was the only way I could sleep; the only way I could drown out the tug of the Holy Spirit on my heart. Even in this horrible state, I would dream about lying at the sawdust strewn altar where I was baptized in the Holy Ghost years before. My hands would be lifted up, and I would be talking in tongues. This would wake me up, and to my shock, the lights in my room would be turned on, and the music was turned off! Then as my mind would clear the lights would be turned down by an unseen hand, and the deathly demonic music would return to its pounding volume. I would lower my upraised hands with my heart racing. The Lord would say, "it's lonely out there isn't it son? You'll be back…"

Those experiences drove me to cut off my ties to the drug culture. I processed out of the military and made my way to Lake Charles, Louisiana, where my parents were pastoring at the time.

The call of God was on my life, and in just a few years, I took the pastorate of my first church. God was moving in my life, and we experienced many signs, miracles, and wonders because we took God at his word and accepted the scriptural declaration that Jesus was the same yesterday, today and forever. I'll never forget the day that a young pastor's daughter from another congregation came with her family to one of our meetings. She came to the altar for prayer (we actually had altar calls in those days). She had discharged from the hospital the day before, and the doctors had called her to come back in immediately. She was diagnosed with an inoperable malignant tumor in her brain. We laid hands on her and commanded healing. She was instantly delivered, and I sent her back to the doctors to verify the diagnosis.

After this lady returned to the doctors to confirm her healing, they had more bad news. Her blood tests revealed a severe strain of hepatitis and on top of that mononucleosis. She was extremely contagious, and they quickly put her in an isolation unit while they considered what treatment regimen to proceed with. About this time, the family reached out to me and asked if I would go to the hospital to pray for her again. I arrived at the hospital and saw her through the double isolation windows the doctors had secluded her behind. I intended to go lay hands on her, but the hospital staff demanded that I put on a gown and mask to protect myself from infection. Anger and boldness rose up in me, as I pushed past them and barged into the isolation room unprotected. I hadn't come there to contract disease I'd come there to heal disease! The woman was instantly healed and discharged the next day completely whole.

Not long after this, another young woman came forward diagnosed with late-stage ovarian cancer. She not only wanted to be healed (obviously) she wanted to have children. In those days, I learned not to hesitate or think too long about the plight of the people coming for prayer. I laid hands on her and declared her healed. I told her to keep her next doctor's appointment, and the confirmation came – she was totally healed with no sign of cancer in her body. That wasn't all. Within a few weeks, she became pregnant with her first child and went on to have five children to her great delight. God was a prayer-answering God, and we were taking him at his word.

The Lord wasn't through demonstrating Himself. The little church was growing even though I was young and inexperienced (only 22 years old at the time). I often joked that the only time I questioned the wisdom of God was when he put such a young and green kid as I was into the ministry. That being the case those years were highlights of the ministry we've walked in now for over 38 years. Time and again in those years, those with hopeless cases and deathbed diagnoses came to our simple storefront church and came away healed by the power of God. Our faith was simple and our expectations high that what the Father said in his word would be our experience, and we were not to be disappointed.

The most significant miracle we saw during those years was after we outgrew our facilities at the time and moved to a bigger building. I got up on Sunday morning and took a text from the book of Colossians:

[Col 2:15 KJV] 15 [And] having spoiled principalities and powers, he made a shew of them openly, triumphing over them in it.

Having read that opening verse, I gave the title of my message to be "Satan is a Defeated Foe." No sooner than the words came out my mouth, an elderly lady on the front row collapsed and pitched onto the floor. It so happened that two RN's were sitting on either side of her and quickly sprang to her aid. After a few moments, they both looked up at me shaking their heads. She was gone. She was dead. The atmosphere in the congregation at that moment was electric with panic and fear. The pews were filled mostly with college students and medical school students from McNeese University. Before they could react, I spoke up:

"Folks, don't move and don't say anything. Just give me 1 minute..."

At that, I knelt and put my hand over the lady's still form. I commanded life to come back into her body. In the name of Jesus, I refused to let her die. I prayed with all the faith I could muster and miraculously she suddenly shook, stirred, gave a great whooping inhalation of air and sat back up in the pew, straightening her glasses with her bible in her lap, glaring at me as though to object that she 'd been made such an object of attention. The kids in the pews jumped up, shouting. They didn't know what else to do. As one man they ran out of the building and down the street screaming at the top of their lungs. They'd experienced the power of God and they as well as ourselves were forever changed.

Chapter Seven

GOD KNOWS MY NAME!

Kitty:

I had only been filled with the Spirit a short period of time when the Father introduced me to the prophetic in a powerful way. I had left the banking business and was trusting in God to provide and show the way to provide for the family and at the same time, be able to be at home with the children. The answer came when He allowed me to watch children and have a daycare in my home. At one point, I had a total of twelve two-year-old's (which was just training for the restaurant He gave me later). This was very demanding of my time, so I hired my neighbor to help, and she was so kind to sit in for me and watch the children so I could go to a morning session of a Women's Aglow meeting in Camarillo, CA. The meeting was at 10 am, and I promised her I would be back by noon to help her with the lunch menu and feeding all the children in my home-based daycare.

A lady came to speak, Lois Burkett, and she was from Sedona, AZ. To emphasize the power of what happened next, I must mention that I had never seen her before. I was unfamiliar with a lot of prophetic stuff at this point, still being young. I really enjoyed the meeting. There were about 200 women, and I was sitting in the back row by the door, so if they were not done, I could slip out quietly and not disturb. Noontime approached, so I quietly made my exit to drive home and help feed the little ones as I promised my helper. After I had left, about 15 or 20 minutes after I was back home, the president of that chapter called me up and said, "Miss Kitty, you will not believe what happened." She said when Lois Burkett finished her message, she concluded and said, "I would like to prophesy to a few people. Ladies, help me out here, is there a Kitty here, or has she gone?" Listening to this report over the phone, I was just swept off my feet by the power of the Holy Ghost. I started weeping, and weeping because here I am, newly spirit-filled, knowing God wants to operate gifts in my life and show Me His multitude of ways of speaking to us, and at that instant, my heart said, "He knows your name Kitty, now you 'know that you know' your name is written in the Lamb's Book of Life." It was such a relief to me, just being the average person, a normal girl, thinking, you kind of wonder sometimes, is it really true, is my name written in heaven? I knew now, most assuredly, it was.

What did Lois have to say after calling my name out? It was fascinating what unfolded because this led to a leadership position I had no idea would come about. Lois called my name, and the president of our chapter said, "Oh, Miss Kitty had to leave at noon." She said, "well, let's just pray in the Holy Ghost." They all went into strong tongues and prayed for a short period.

There was a strong sense she had heard from God, but she wouldn't release what she was seeing. Nonetheless, they were all in agreement in the tongues, but I didn't know any of this was happening. Hearing the report by phone, I was just so relieved to know, God knew my name. As it turns out, I was asked to serve in the position of treasurer of our Aglow chapter because I had been a banker for many years.

Enjoying that position, about three or four weeks later, a question came up about renewing the other leadership positions for that chapter. I had been appointed because the last treasurer had stepped aside and I was finishing the term. I'm vacuuming my floor one morning, and I hear the Father say, "If you were called to the office of the president, would you be willing to serve?" I said, "you mean treasurer, right God? Treasurer." He said, "If you were called to the office of the president, would you be willing to serve?" I fell on my knees, turned off the vacuum, and just cried like a baby. I said, "Yes, sir, I will do anything for you. I will go in there and clean their toilets if I have to, I just want to serve you with my whole life." About maybe three more weeks go by, and I get a phone call and it's the president of the Aglow chapter again, whose name was Evelyn. She said, "Kitty if you were called to the office of the president, would you be willing to serve?" In tears, I said, "Yes!" The Father already told me, and I just knew it was Him. I didn't know all that the position entails but I said yes." She said, "Praise the Lord, we have fasted for a week, and the Lord said, that Kitty was the next president of the Aglow Chapter in Camarillo, CA." That was my first huge dose of exercising the gifts that were in me, and I didn't even know what you would call them. I just knew I loved Jesus, and I could tell others what He told me and it would be just that way. Then I would I pray again, and He would speak and the demonstration of His Spirit would come forth and bless someone, and I would move on to the next adventure.

That word about serving in the office of the president would come back around a few years later. In my restaurant days which I will include in another chapter – there was a little papa around 80 years old who came with a word for me. We were in a tent revival, and he approached me. He was an uncle of a real close Spirit-filled lady friend, and I knew he was a reliable follower of Jesus. My friend had talked about him and his prophecies in the past. After I ministered one night in the tent revival, we had set up out in the parking lot of my restaurant, Mr. Ray walked up to me and said, "Miss Kitty, I have a word for you from the Father, but may I whisper it in your ear because it's kind of unusual?" I said, "Of course you can, Ray." He pulls me aside and said, "One day, you are going to prophesy to the President of the United States of America." When Mr. Ray whispered that in my ear, I heard that word given years before pop back up in my spirit, "If you were called to the office of the president, would you be willing to serve?" I knew it had meant more than just that initial office in the Women's Aglow chapter. One other time beyond that, somebody prophesied to me years later, "I see you prophesying to the President of the United States." I said, "Ok, that's awesome." You can't bring a word like that (or any word for that matter) to pass. You just have to receive the word, believe the prophets, and keep living for Jesus. Time has passed, and yet that word continues to be confirmed over and again. Just a few weeks before writing these words, our mentor prophet who we have learned to love and respect all these years, Walter Waller, was greeting us and having a meal with us in Oklahoma City. As is his custom, he was prophesying away, telling us those things that God was laying on his heart to share. He was talking about this next property that we are going to get is just a stepping stone to something larger, which in our hearts we believe is that 750 acres, $7.5 million just a few miles on the other side of this property we are looking at right now in Green Valley, AZ. He continued, "I see the president is going to come to the property. He's going to need to talk to you, and you're going to need to talk to him. The president is going to come and be before you and be with you." And we know that just like the prophetic word that came, "If you were called to the office of the president, would you be willing to serve?" As that word came to pass years ago, just assuredly what others have shared and what Walter shared will likewise one day come to pass.

Always remember – Jesus knows your name!

Chapter Eight

RESURRECTED AND TRANSLATED A 100 MILES

Russs:

After pastoring in south and central Louisiana for many years, I was offered a position with a small denomination headquartered in southeast Missouri. While there I worked as head of the evangelism department and was also responsible for the publishing work, producing many titles for the founder of our organization and also writing Christian education resources for use in this group's youth programs and bible school. It was during my time here that I initially met Kitty while she was pastoring one of the churches (in Seymour, Missouri) associated with our parent organization. Shortly after preaching for Kitty, the Lord began to prepare me to make an exit from denominational work. Initially, I saw working for this group as a promotion to greater ministry but found to my disappointment it was no more than a bureaucratic office with no meaningful outlet for the call of God I felt upon my life. I prayed long and hard for God to open a door of escape for me, and one day, my answer came in the form of a prophetic word.

My eldest brother was living in the Kansas City area at the time, and he visited a church were a prophet friend of mine by the name of Gene Bacon was ministering. He called him up to the front and holding a cassette recorder in his hand gave a word that was not intended for my brother but myself. The declaration was that my time working for the denomination was drawing to a close and a door of opportunity was about to open. My brother received the word and called me up to play the recording over the phone. I was relieved and blessed to know that something was about to shift. That very next day a minister by the name of Floyd Achord called me up. Floyd was credentialled as an evangelist with our organization, but he had a strong prophetic anointing on his life. As we spoke on the phone that day, Floyd repeated almost word for word what Gene Bacon had prophesied. Not only did Bro. Achord prophesy that I would be leaving the position I was in with the denomination, he also put his money where his mouth was and pledged $2500 to help me make the move to wherever God would send me. Shortly after that, I made the move to Windsor, Missouri.

My natural father had retired from active ministry after 38 years as a pastor. He moved to this little town of Windsor and opened a business and bought several investment properties. When God released me from the denomination, He instructed me to relocate where my parents were now retired and to assist them in anything, they needed help with. This was in the mid-'90s, and for the first time in many years I was moving from full-time ministry after pastoring two churches and working as a denominational leader, I would now foray into the business world in order to care for my family and fulfill the mandate of the Father to be a support to my dad. I went into the computer business, and after a rocky start God really opened the doors of blessing up to me, and I continued in this work through the 1990s until 2010 when I turned the business over to my eldest son who still runs it today.

While working in the business world, my father helped me buy an older Victorian home on Main street in Windsor. It was a 15-room structure that was built in the mid-1800s with high ceilings and the unique character of a house that was over 100 years old. It sat on a one-acre lot in the middle of town and after settling in my near neighbor down the street named Billy came for a visit. Billy was a disabled diesel mechanic suffering from a myriad of illnesses arising from a life of dissipation and alcoholism. His liver was failing. Diabetes was ravaging his body. His heart was compromised, as well. He was in and out of the doctor's care yet all this time he continual sought us out as his neighbor to be a blessing to us in any way he could.

Billy was illiterate and very simple-minded, yet he loved us with all his heart. He was ten years older than I was, but he still chose to call me "Dad," and there wasn't a chore or handyman task around our house that Billy wasn't quick to identify the need and take care of things all the while refusing any payment for doing so. I was touched by Billy's love for the family and shared Jesus with him many times to no avail. I would give him the gospel, and he would just hang his head and say, "well, you know Dad, I'm just not a religious fellow..." I was frustrated by his continual rebuffs all the while his love for my family and servants' heart just continued on unabated.

After several years Billy's health deteriorated, and I recieved word he had been taken by ambulance to the Research Medical hospital in Kansas City. The general consensus of the doctors was that Billy was facing end-of-life and wouldn't likely be coming home soon or at all for that matter. One night after dinner, the phone rang. It was the RN on duty calling from Billy's room to inform us at his request that things didn't look good. Whispering in a low tone the RN gave me to understand that the doctor didn't think that Billy would last out the night and further that Billy had asked her to call so I could pray for him. My thoughts were that now at last Billy would be ready to accept Jesus as his savior.

The RN handed Billy the phone, and I commenced to pray one of those end-of-life prayers that I had prayed so many times before as a pastor. Billy, however, would have none of it. He wasn't ready to die, and he made it plain to me that he wanted me to pray to God that he would come home and carry on with his life. I was a little frustrated because I wanted to pray Billy into heaven, and Billy just wasn't cooperating. In the back of my mind, I asked God what I should do. The Lord's voice came loud and clear that I was to pray the best prayer I knew how to pray asking that Billy would be raised up to new life, completely healed and whole and come home totally restored. I prayed exactly that, but to be honest, I questioned what the outcome would really be. After a few more words of comfort, I hung up the phone and thought that was the end of that, and we would hear soon that Billy was in heaven. This was not to be the case.

What happened next is one of those things that if it hadn't happened to me, I wouldn't believe it. In relaying this story to you, I give you permission to doubt what I'm going to tell you at the same time assuring you that without embellishment or exaggeration this was exactly what took place. About thirty minutes after hanging up the phone with Billy, there came a knock at the door. I opened the door, and to my confusion, Billy was standing on my front porch wearing nothing but a ball cap and a hospital gown and nothing else. It was freezing cold out, so I pulled him in the house and sat him down, wrapping my overcoat over his shoulders.

"Billy," I asked, "how did you get here?" In the back of my mind, I was trying to grasp what was happening because I just hung up with Billy dying in a hospital room 98 miles away. That's right – 98 miles away, but somehow only 30 minutes later Billy was standing at my front door in a very curious state of dress. I just couldn't figure it out, so I continued asking questions. Billy was confused himself and seemed to be drifting off in his mind while I pressed him for an explanation as to why he was here at my house, where were his clothes and how did he travel

100 miles from the hospital to my house in only 30 minutes!

"How did you get here, Billy?" I asked.

"Well, them men brought me, dad…"

"What men are you talking about Billy?"

"Why them men that took the sheet off my head…"

Instantly my mind grasped that certainly, Billy had died and the hospital staff put him in the morgue. But who were these men that took the sheet off of him and how on earth did he get here to my house in under 30 minutes?

"You mean the paramedics, right, Billy?"

"I don't know Dad. They just walked me out of the hospital and put me in their car…"

In my mind, I still can't make sense of what Billy is saying. "You mean they took you out on a gurney and brought you in an ambulance?" I was still calculating the time even the fastest ambulance with lights and sirens could transport Billy to my house and why would they do that in the first place. Billy continued to explain:

"No, they weren't paramedics, Dad and they didn't put me on a gurney or take me in an ambulance."

"What do you mean, Billy? What kind of car did they bring you in?"

I couldn't decipher what Billy's recollections were, and none of it made sense, but Billy answered: "I've never seen a car like this one, Dad…"

The confusion deepened. "Did they say anything to you, Billy?"

"No Dad, they didn't say anything to me – they just asked each other if they thought I knew what was going on."

I was astounded. Billy hadn't been brought to my door by any conveyance I could imagine. The two men must have been angels who took Billy out of the morgue and brought him supernaturally to my front door in a mere 30 minutes when the drive was over 100 miles! I sent someone down to his house a few doors down for some clothes, and we walked him back and got him settled in his own bed for the night. Over the next few days, Billy returned to his local doctor who pronounced that Billy had no signs of liver failure, no signs of diabetes and was in fact in perfect health. There was no explanation as to how he recovered so miraculously or how he was supernaturally transported to my front door late in the night with such an amazing report to give of angels escorting him from death to total deliverance in Jesus' name.

After all these fantastic things, Billy turned his heart to the Lord. He couldn't read so I gave him the bible on CD to listen to. I would come home from work, and Billy would be sitting on my porch, ready to talk about God. "You know Dad; I was up last night –

talkin'…" That's what Billy called prayer as he didn't have any religious background to share from. He would tell me what the Lord laid on his heart, and we would pray together and rejoice in the touch of God on his life. To my knowledge years later, Billy is still alive to tell his amazing and wonderful story.

Chapter Nine

SEYMOUR SIGNS AND WONDERS

Kitty:

You will remember that I came up on the west coast all my early life. My parents had raised us six kids, mostly in California, but one day they wanted to see one of my sisters who married a guy she met Germany named Bill Hubbard who lived in Marshfield, MO. Mom and Dad said that we were going on vacation to see where Kris, my sister, was living out on this farm in rural Missouri. Now, my dad was born in Hurley, Missouri, so visiting back in the Midwest was a real homecoming for him. When he came back to California, we could see he fell in love with his roots all over and again. Shortly after he announced to the family, he was leaving California for Missouri because, "I need to be there," he said, because it felt right to him, so he made a move to a little town called Seymour, Missouri.

In this little town where mom and dad settled, there was a restaurant called "Miss Kitty's." We laughed when dad told us about the restaurant that he was going down to "Miss Kitty's" to have some biscuits and gravy." It was a restaurant that was sitting there on the corner of this little tiny town with only three entrances into it. Dad would tell us all about it and say, "when you get a chance you guys come out here for a vacation, you see how pretty it is."

At first, I was unconvinced. I said, "Dad, where is Missouri? I don't even know where Missouri is!"

I kid you not I was a "valley girl" from California before they had valley girls. I had to get out a map and look it up because I didn't know where it was. Eventually, we drove out from the west coast for a visit, and arriving in Seymour, dad just told me to take this the middle entrance into town when we came for a summer vacation. The day came, and we piled the kids in the car and went on vacation to see why my mom and dad were so happy in a place called Missouri. In the meantime, my eldest sister and my youngest sister moved to Seymour to be near my parent. (Seymour, by the way, is spelled the same as "William Seymour," the founder of the Azuza street revival.) So, we're pulling into town, and dad had said to "turn onto Division Street" and there off of Highway 60 up on a hill, on the corner, there was Miss Kitty's Restaurant with a 12 x 12 "For Sale" sign on the side of it. Instantly my spirit leapt within me, and the Father said, "You're going to buy that restaurant," and I said "what?" The Father's voice I knew so well repeated, "You're going to buy that restaurant; it's what you been asking me for." What an amazing thing, and it already had my name on it "Miss Kitty's Family Restaurant." Shortly after that, we bought the restaurant that had been on the market

2 ½ years just waiting for us to come along and fulfill God's plan for that season by making it our own.

So one day, we're hanging around doing the family thing, and it's such a small town that they have something called "the square," and for those of you who don't know or have never been on a square it's just that, it's only a little central area in many small towns that had a square in its layout. Most often the courthouse is in the middle. On Friday and Saturday nights the kids would cruise the square (as they called it). It was the happening place to be so one afternoon we decided to walk up to the square and see who we might meet. We went to the little grocery store in town to buy some snacks and a cold drink. When I went to check out and got up to the clerk (whose name is Judy.) Judy then says to me, "Hi! Who are you? Who is your mama? Who is your daddy?" and when she said that I got this big lump in my throat and tears in my eyes because in California you could go through the grocery line and they would say "how you doing?" and one might answer "Well I'm dying of cancer thank you very much..." And then they would say "have a great day" because they didn't hear you because they didn't want to listen to you, they were too busy. Here in Seymour, I had this hunger and heart for people to connect, and Judy didn't know it, but she was pulling on my heartstrings. In answer to her question, I told her who my Father was (named Vern), and she said, "Oh, yes, and Karen is your sister, Shirley's her daughter..." I just was beside myself with joy, knowing what I heard coming into town.

It was about three days into the visit with my folks, and I told them that I believed we're supposed to buy Miss Kitty's and they were all happy. Even though I didn't have any restaurant experience, I did have people in my home very often, and they would end up around our dinner table. Now on a side note, be aware that I don't love to cook, but I was willing to do so to have a chance to tell others about Jesus. Without any experience, I made an offer on the restaurant they accepted it! I then said, "Well, we need to find a house - let's go look for a house." There were many available, but we wanted something close to the main road. We were not familiar with driving in snow and ice, so we looked for a place with easy in and out and access to that highway. As we were driving down the road, I saw a beautiful ranch style for sale by the owner. As I observed the house from the highway, I said, "turn in here, I like that house." The home was beautiful! The house was recently built and owned by a man named Mr. Pool who at that moment we saw putting his lawnmower in the garage as we pulled into the driveway.

I introduced myself and said, "this is our house IS our house" I had it by the Holy Spirit. We ended up getting it at a fantastic price for around $70,000. It was a brand-new build with 4000 ft. with an upstairs-downstairs, on 6 acres. Now all that was left to do was to return to California, sell that house and make a move. Things moved quickly. A man from New York City who worked for Apple computers bought our place sight unseen. We got the full asking price that we wanted, which was around $145,000 – a nice windfall to finance the move and the transition from West Coast living to run a restaurant in the rural Midwest.

As we were packing up the truck and getting ready roll to Missouri, I ask the Lord, "Why Missouri, why Seymour, Missouri? I would have gone to Russia, China, or anywhere for you if you had just asked..." To which the Father replied, "I want them to "see-more signs and wonders" and demonstrations of my Spirit, and it's called the 'Show me state.'" (I had no idea that this was the state motto at the time). He went on, "I promise you; I will show my power; I will display my glory because you already give me credit for everything I do." So, I was just in awe of that statement of 'Seymour signs and wonders,' and I did know about William J Seymour at the time and I felt there was a spiritual connection that would bring about a great testimony in time to come.

In regards to the owning a restaurant, I figured I could learn the operations of what was done there by working with the owners until escrow closed on it, and they agreed. They paid me two dollars an hour to work for them eight hours a day (which was a little bit hard on my flesh). However, I knew I was investing by faith. I was trained for about a month in the restaurant and in the kitchen also and how to take orders and all the other things needed to run an eatery. It wasn't long before the "Seymour signs and wonders" started in full force.

It was during the first winter we were there that a

81

great miracle took place that was actually written in a book it was so unusual. I had just taken the turkey out of the oven and was warming the rolls for Thanksgiving dinner, and a power outage struck our area taking out all power for over 45 miles around. I had my family there my Mother, Father, sisters, brother and their spouses and children and I just pulled the food out of the oven, and the power went down, and we said, "oh maybe It will come right back", because we've experienced that in California but it didn't come right back. The phone rang, and it was a lady who lived across the street from our restaurant calling me and said, "Miss Kitty you're going to want to go down to the restaurant" (I lived 3 miles away down the highway) The neighbor continued to inform me "… your lights are burning, and you don't want to have that electricity bill be high if you're not going to be there.", I said, "what do you mean"? And she said, "Yes, Kitty all the lights are on in your restaurant." She then asked if I had a generator, and I said, "no ma'am." We went to see what was going on and sure enough, my place of business had power and lights even though not one bit of electricity was available for a 45-mile radius!

The signs and wonders that God promised were beginning to happen. Standing in my warm, well-lit restaurant, I remembered what the Father said: "I am going to make you a lighthouse that is set on a hill that cannot be hidden. I just knew God was up to something. When I got to the restaurant the next day, people started turning on to the property to get gas (we had gas pumps on that property) and to get food.

We turned on the grills and went to work and for six days we were slammed with customers. One right after another, with whole groups of people coming in to get gas which I just had the tanks filled, and food to which I had stocked up on because I had just had a grocery truck delivery. These droves of people would come to our place hearing from their friends that we had power, food, and gas, so they were lined up and down the street and around the block from long distances for food and to buy fuel from us.

About the second day, we hosted three co-ops of electricians from companies coming together to figure out what was going on and to locate the problem. One of the foremen came up to my counter to pay and he said "you're Miss Kitty aren't you" Standing there in my frilly apron I replied, "well, yes sir I am" to which he replied, "you must have a pretty big generator to have this place going like it is..." I replied, "Sir I don't have a generator... oh, wait! I do have a generator but not the kind you might think! I serve the Father of lights, the Lord God Almighty and He promised me I was going to be a lighthouse on the hill and not be hidden, and so I give him credit for it".

"You see," I continued, "we pray before we get in trouble around here." That rough old boss man started to cry, tears running down his face. "I'm going to start praying right now, Miss Kitty." Six days later, the power came back on. During the six days of the outage, we had to bring family members into the restaurant to keep it running and had extra loads of groceries brought out from Springfield which was 30 miles away as God blessed us and we blessed the people. This miraculous event has even been written about because it was such a miracle.

That initial breakthrough established our business not just to feed people but to preach, teach, and prophesy about the goodness of God. The term "marketplace ministry" wasn't around at that time, but that is precisely what I was walking in. People would come in our doors, turn and say to me, "I have never been in here before," and I would say, "well why are you in here today"? They would reply with, "I don't know something just told me to stop here today," and with that, I would say, "well I have a pretty good idea so let's just visit a little bit." I would then get acquainted with them and listen to what the Holy Spirit had to say, and they responded beautifully. One day, I had a full dining room, and I did not have another server, so it was just myself out there with 52 seats. I would turn in orders in by clipping them on the wheel positioned on the pass through between the dining area and the kitchen and say "order," and when the foods were ready they would yell "pick up, pick up" and so I would bring the food out to the people.

One day I walked up to this table by the window on the highway side, and this elderly gentleman and his wife are sitting in the booth, and I said, "May I help you?" I was talking through a somewhat hurried tone because I had a full dining room and no backup. The old fellow looked up at me with anguish in his eyes "you a preacher ain't ya"? And I said "yes sir I am," He replied "well then you better pray" and as soon as he said those words I saw a dark cloud over this man's head with my spiritual eyes, and I knew instantly it was a spirit of death. I said "Sir, come with me, ma'am come with me" I was in a hurry because of all the customers, but the prompting of the Holy Ghost gave me no other option but to take the time to minister to this forlorn little papa. I led the couple through the swinging café doors, through the kitchen, back by the noisy chicken fryer we had at the time and I asked him "Sir what has happened to you recently that you wish to die"? And then his wife just started sobbing, and he starts to cry, and he exclaimed, "I recently retired, and nobody wants me, and nobody needs me for anything. I'm so desperate, and I don't know what to do". Speaking by the inspiration of God, I shot back "Sir, you have children"? He replies, "Yes" I question him again, "you have grandchildren?" And he says, "Yes." So, I said, "you can't die, you have to live to declare the goodness of God to your children and grandchildren. You have an assignment, and I break the curse of death over you in the name of Jesus Christ, and I set you free from the bondage of death, and you will live and not die, and you will declare the works of the Lord!

The entire conversation took about 90 seconds and all the while the bell was ringing, and the staff knows I'm back there, but the bell is ringing "pick up pick up pick up," and after a few seconds I just turned to the two cooks and said, "take the food out"! Obeying God took precedence over anything else, and the result averted a tragedy for that little family. Another example was regarding woman contemplating suicide. She dropped in, and I got to speak with her and share the good news of Jesus Christ. In my restaurant, I had gospel tracts on my tables, from End-Time Handmaidens. In eight years, 35,000 "Who is Jesus" pamphlets went out the door, taken because people were hungry to know the truth. Some people would look up, and they'd have their food before them, and I would see from across the dining room that they would have tears running down their face. Sometimes I would speak to them if I was prompted, and if not, I would let the Word do the work and lives were changed.

One morning I woke about 6 AM with these words sounding off in my spirit "get up and pray. Judy is suicidal." I knew the voice of God when I heard it and replied, "yes, sir!" I hurried out of bed and started praying and taking authority over the situation. As soon as I got around to finishing that prayer, the Lord told me to call her. I picked up the phone and rang Judy's number: "Judy, it's Kitty, the thing you have in your heart to do is not of God, the enemy is trying to take you out right before you get the dream of a lifetime coming true to you! I take authority over that spirit of death and the curse of death that is trying to come over you, and I set you free in the name of Jesus".

On the other end of the line, Judy is sobbing and sobbing. "What are you doing Judy"? She said, "I was sitting here by the side of my bed planning my suicide, and I was trying to figure out how to do it so that my dad wouldn't be so upset and distraught." I spoke life and hope to her in the name of the Lord, and she realized what a mistake it was and she got set free from that. Judy was 58 at that time and was a spinster. She was a single child, had never been married, and was a farm girl who had always helped her parents on the farm. Her mother had passed, and her daddy was living with her, and she was caring for him and working at the market. Well, in a matter of a few months a man came to town in Missouri who was from Connecticut, and he fell head over heels in love with Judy, and Judy fell in love with him, and so her highest heart's desire was satisfied such a blessing.

Chapter Ten

THE THREE MISSING
WOMEN CASE:

Kitty:

In moving to Missouri, the Lord assured me that He would show signs and wonders in the "Show Me" state and that He would show His power and display His glory. There came a moment during my restaurant days that this promise of God would be carried out in the revealing of a mystery regarding three women who were kidnapped in nearby Springfield, Missouri.

I had moved to Missouri in 1986, and during the restaurant days, I was keeping busy running mostly the front part of the restaurant while the cooks were working in the back-preparing meals for the diners who would come my way. This was ideal because I was able to be with the people and testify of my Lord and Savior Jesus Christ. So, under this arrangement, I was the server full-time and only part-time cooking to relieve the cooks in the kitchen.

During that time, the news came on that that three women had been abducted in the city of Springfield, which was 30 miles away from our home. They had been kidnapped without a trace. All that was left of them was their purses, their keys, and their personal possessions found in the house. It was a mother and a daughter and the daughter's best friend; who had just that day graduated from high school in Springfield. The girls were planning on going to Silver Dollar City (a nearby amusement park) the next day to celebrate. That day of fun would never take place because sometime in the night they were abducted. At first, nobody knew what had happened, because they were just gone leaving everything behind (keys, purses, etc.). There was widespread news coverage as authorities strived to figure out what had happened to this mom and two high school grads.

About two weeks into the investigation I was watching the news when I saw psychics get on and talk about 'well we think this, and we think that' and so on. Hearing that began to infuriate me in my spirit because our Father knows everything, He has eyes to see and ears to hear. So, I turned right then to my cook, and said to him, "will you just agree with me right now that God will tell his prophets where these missing women are, what happened, and it will somehow be settled, but God will get all the glory?"

I just knew in my heart this was how this had to play out because after all the Father did tell me this was the "Show Me" state and that He promised to show his power to display his glory.

Right there in the kitchen of my café, we prayed believing God that things were going to shift and that

He would move in this situation. Four hours later, I came back from making the day's bank deposit when my daughter Jennifer said, "Mom, you need to call Miss Laura." Miss Laura was a godly lady friend of the family that lived about 40 miles away. My daughter Jennifer went on to say, "Miss Laura said she needs to talk to you right away." I said, "ok." I stole a moment between busy meal times at the diner and made the phone call.

"Laura, it's Kitty, what's going on?" I did not hesitate to take Laura seriously because I knew her because she was psalmist who sang some beautiful worship and praise music and I had been in several meetings with her, so I knew her character, I knew her spirit was true and pure. Miss Laura replied over the phone:

"Miss Kitty I had an open vision of the three missing women, and I know exactly what happened to them, but before I tell you what happened in the vision, I want to tell you a couple of things that God has done in my life just to let you be at peace."

As she continued sharing with me, I had goosebumps on top of goosebumps, because the Holy Spirit was confirming that she was speaking from the true spirit of God and that she was operating under His spirit. She went on to say, "Miss Kitty, as God is my witness, it was like somebody ran a videotape through my living room, as I sat up through the night as God showed me the details of the case that were yet to be made known - this scenario, these scenes, these details and secrets regarding the fate of these three women. She then proceeded to tell me that the women were abducted and they were murdered and drowned in the Lake of the Ozarks, which was in the central part of the state.

She continued and said it had to do with prostitution and pornography. She revealed that she saw a boat with the name of "Cindy's Pride" or "Cindy Pride" on it. There were also three names of three men and also saw some letters on the boat as well. She also said she saw a phone number and a street address with which she had all written down. She said she had checked the names and the phone numbers and one of the phone numbers turned out to be the last four phone digits to reach the detective who was assigned to the case.

So here I was listening to her tell me this story with all these confirmations, and she said, "I even went so far as to look up boat registrations in Missouri, and there was one that said Cindy's Pride. She then researched the number and name on that boat (Cindy's Pride), and she said that the Holy Spirit prompted her even before she called me to look this up and she found it as the Holy Spirit lead her, and she called the phone number. When someone answered, she said, "Hi, I was wondering if you still have the boat for sale"? The voice on the other end of the line said, "how did you know we had a boat for sale"?

"Well," she goes on, "do you have it or not"? Then the voice on the end of the line told her "it's already sold," and slammed the phone down very angrily.

Hearing all of this with great amazement I then proceeded to tell Laura that this morning, four hours ago, I was standing in the restaurant and I said, "Father you know what happened to those women, you have eyes to see, and ears to hear. You promised you were going to show your power and display your glory; I think this kidnapping case would be a great opportunity, would you just tell your prophets? Would you just tell your prophets like Brother Hagan, and they could prophesy, and say this is what God says about this case to silence the psychics and the clairvoyants?"

Why did I pray this way? Because since I was a little girl, my motive has always been redemption. I want to lead people to Jesus. If in fact, it was going to be these people that murdered and took advantage of these women and murdered them at the end, I just knew that God could redeem them. Yes, these people who did this are really bad people, but God sent Jesus to die for everyone, and in my heart I'm thinking we can still minister to them and say listen, "God knows, God saw, and He will forgive you, if you just come back to him."

I then asked Laura, "Laura, why did you call and tell me this?" To which she said, "because God told me you're his preacher and you have been preaching since you were a little girl and this will preach especially when everybody sees and hears that God knows more than the psychics," and I said, "You are absolutely right."

Now, the next thing to happen was, in walked one of my customers named Elijah Trantham who was from West Plains, Missouri, about 60 miles away. He and his wife Bernie sat down in my booth, and we would always have coffee together if I had some free time. During those moments, we would visit and talk about the Holy Spirit, about the Word. Elijah is sitting in my booth, and I checked with the Father, and I asked, "Father, can I ask Elijah to hear me out on the missing women case?"

At the time, I did not know I was prophetic; I was just trying to obey God as I had since I was a little girl. The Father then said, "Yes, go ask Elijah." I went over to him and his wife and told them what happened. Tears welled up in both of their eyes he said, "Kitty, this is God, and I can tell you feel strongly about this. Number one, don't talk to anybody about this if God does not sanction it. He doesn't want you just to spill your beans to just anybody." I could feel the seriousness of it myself. He went on to say, "Furthermore I want to tell you that I have a friend who owns a boat company in the Lake of the Ozarks." He then told me about a man named Larry Ollison, who had three companies, one of which was called Raymond Boat Sales. Elijah went on to say, "I feel like you're supposed to talk to him." I then thanked him, and I said to God, "Thank you, Father, I know you are all over this."

Now, Laura lived 45 miles away so she's not there at

that moment, but I'm just beginning to track the Holy Ghost (Russ calls me his scratch and sniff prophet. If I see or hear Jesus, Holy Spirit or the Father anywhere I am going after it). The next thing I did was I called Raymond Boat Sales and asked to speak to Larry Ollison (who is also the pastor of Walk on the Water Faith Church at the Lake of the Ozarks).

An elderly lady answered, and I said, "Hi, may I please speak to Larry Ollison" and she said, "Honey Larry is out of town, he's in Tulsa till Wednesday." She continued to explain, "But I'm his mom, sweetie, so if you want to tell me, I will get the message to him and have him call you when he gets back to town." I then told her that it was a somewhat sensitive issue and that it had to do with the three missing women. She replied, "Miss Kitty, trust me our telephone lines, fax lines, and everything here is secure, and you'll be in a really safe environment if you want to share with me, and then I can accurately tell him why you need him to call you." I told her, and she said she would give him the message just as soon as possible and she reminded me that he would be back in town on Wednesday. I didn't have to wait that long for that very night my phone rings, and it's Larry Ollison calling from Tulsa Oklahoma, which is four hours from my home and restaurant.

"Miss Kitty, I don't know exactly what you all have to share with me, but if you will just tell me what it is on your heart. I feel that God is in this and have from the time this afternoon that I heard it from my mom ".

We then had the discussion, in more detail than I gave his mother about what Laura had seen and had confirmed already on her own. He then replied, "this is so interesting and wild that you would tell me this, and you wouldn't have known this, but I am the president of the state water patrol board, and I have jurisdiction over every waterway in the state of Missouri."

I wasn't really surprised at this because like Russ always says you can't make this stuff up only God can orchestrate it. We're talking about miracles signs and wonders for the glory of God and the redemption for humanity.

Larry continued, "This morning I was approached by the press, bombarding me and asking 'Mr. Ollison, what do you know about the prostitution and pornography ring that was just broken up on your lake jurisdiction'? To which he replied he didn't know anything about it.

So, Kitty, what you're telling me and what just what happened to me makes evident that there is a connection between us and I know God is in it". He then said, "I have a friend who is a chief investigator for the state water patrol whose name is Jim Marlin and I would like him to call you, and you can tell him exactly what you told me."

 A few days go by, and Mr. Marlin calls and says, "Hi Miss Kitty! I got this message, and it's very intriguing to me." I then interjected and said, "Mr. Marlin before you go any further are you a Christian?" To which he replies, "Well, I am a Methodist and this sort of made me pause and take notice that something bigger than my Methodist background is going on here."

He then asked if Laura and I were willing he would like us to go with him to the place that Laura and I had already tracked out from what she had seen in the Spirit. Laura and I had found the location by land previously but hadn't gone out on the water. When we had gotten there, she had just stopped in her tracks and began to weep with her hands raised to heaven, and she said, "This is the very spot." As it turned out that landing was precisely where the prostitution and pornography ring was broken up that week.

The investigator continued, "if you could meet me, we will have a water patrol boat, and we will bring a diver. Every time water patrol comes to the lake everyone sees what is happening so I want you ladies to meet us on the opposite side of the lake several miles away so you will not be connected by onlookers to what is going on. We will pick you and Laura up on the other side of the lake, and we will boat around to the area in question".

At this point, The Holy Spirit said Kitty, "I want you to call the head intercessor at Kenneth Copeland Ministries because (I had been partners with Kenneth Copeland ministries for years and years) I want to have them pray a covering over you." I made a phone call, and I asked to please speak to the head person of their prayer department. They then transferred me to this lady who introduces herself as Nikki Turner. I told her, "Miss Nikki, I'd really appreciate prayer, and I told her that we were partners for a long time, and we needed prayer covering." After hearing the whole story, Nikki replied: "Kitty, I know this is God." She was in tears as I told her how God wanted to reveal himself as God in the Show-Me state. I told her all the parts up to that point, including all the details. I told her about Elijah, Larry Ollison, Jim Marlin and how we had to go on the lake but we needed prayer.

Nikki assured me that prayers would be going up and that there was nothing hidden that would not be revealed and there was nothing done in secret that wouldn't be shouted from the rooftop, even the roof of your mouth (she declared). I thanked her, and before we got off the phone, I said, "Nikki, could I ask how I could pray for you" because that's my custom, when you find someone who is walking with you and you are connecting in the Spirit, it's a two way thing, giving and receiving. Nikki replied said, "well, I have to go to Switzerland with my husband." I said, "why are you dreading going there?" She said, "because my husband's family are strongly religious, and it's challenging." I encouraged her, "well I have a little key that maybe you could pray about and then just have this breakthrough to bring breakthrough to them." I began to talk to her about breaking the curse of the vow of poverty, which will be in another chapter of the book.

The day came then to go to the lake. Laura and I were rejoicing with such a time with our Papa God, knowing that He can do anything He wants, anytime He wants and doesn't have to check in with anybody. We are driving up there rejoicing, and we go to the place where they told us to park. We get out of the car to find Jim waiting on us. When we walked onto the dock we saw it wasn't just Mr. Marlin in a boat; there was also a driver and a diver. There were also five other water patrol boats and five dive teams. There were other people on the boats as well to assist. Jim and said, "We are just going to slowly cruise around to the other side of the lake. While we are going, I would like for you two ladies to tell us exactly how all of this started. Tell us your story because it is quite interesting to us or we wouldn't be here today."

I told him my part, all the way back to why God brought me to Seymour, MO to see more signs and wonders, to the Show-Me State, where God would show His power and display His glory. As we are talking, it's like Jesus is manifesting Himself on that patrol boat. As we approached the spot where God revealed the bodies had been tossed overboard, Jim sent the other boats ahead to hold back traffic as we approach. The closer we got, the more powerful the presence of God came upon us all. They were getting goosebumps with all the hairs on the heads of the divers, driver and Jim the lead investigator standing straight up. All this time, Laura is describing what God had shown her. The bodies were bound to heavy cement pieces with big heavy chains and cast into the lake.

At that point, Mr. Marlin said, "This is the deepest,

darkest lake in the state. A divers can only see three feet in front of you; it's so pitch black. Just so you know that, and it's the deepest, darkest lake in the state. Just bear that in mind in case we don't' see what we're looking for today, trust me, someone will come back because there is so much area to search." We got closer and closer with Laura saying "a little left, a little right," as she was giving instructions. All of a sudden, I felt God in the boat again, and Laura whispers, "we're really really close."

Now picture this, Laura is standing at the front of the boat. It's an open boat maybe 24 feet long. She's standing up holding onto that rail; I'm sitting down next to the investigator in the back. As we approach this area, you could feel the Spirit of God just build and build. As soon as we hit the spot, her knees buckled, and I stood straight up. I didn't even plan on it. I just stood straight up because God was in the boat with us and it was a confirmation of the area that many yards out in the water. The diver and driver are like "what is this?" because they felt it too – something other than natural forces were at work as God was testifying to His power and glory out on the lake as we came near to the depths where the bodies had been discarded by those who took their lives.

Jim then dropped a marker and called all the boats in with their sonar to start scanning the area. One boat came near and picked up the marker Jim had left. I asked Mr. Marlin why they just picked up our marker off of the water, he replied that they detected some anomalies on the lake floor and they didn't have enough markers, so they were borrowing the ones that were closer in because of the reading on their depth finders. They then had divers suit up and do some diving. They were down about forty minutes or so, and they found several things in those areas but not what we were looking for.

Frustrated, I made the observation, "well, they moved the marker." He said, "Don't worry, the very fact that you were willing to come and do this and what we have experienced here on this boat today, tells us we will be bringing other divers out, but you won't have to be involved in it now that we have an idea of where." So, they did their part. When we to the car to go home after this encounter, I said, "Mr. Marlin, we would appreciate knowing when you confirm these things." He said, "you know, being as sensitive as it is, law enforcement, we aren't even allowed to tell anyone till the investigation is over."

The next thing to take place was a divinely orchestrated connection with the lead investigator on the case whose name was Doug Thomas in Springfield, Missouri. Doug happened to be a member of a spirit-filled church in Springfield. We made an inquiry and said we have some information that we feel would be important for you to look into. Doug's response was, "Do me a favor, write all of your details down and the connection with Mr. Ollison and Mr. Marlin, and put every detail you have in writing. I promise you, if you send it to me, my attention only, I will review it, and we will have a meeting at an appropriate time."

We did as Doug requested, rejoicing because we have obeyed and put the package in the mail the next day. In just a few days we get a phone call. Mr. Doug Thomas said, "Can you ladies come in? I want to talk to you in person." I said, "Absolutely." We were excited. We didn't start this, you can't make it happen, and you can't finish it, it is only God doing this stuff. So, we were just rejoicing, as we always have been to obey the Lord when we hear his voice. So, we go into his office and sit down in his cubicle that is soundproof so nobody could listen to us. He wanted the same thing the other investigator wanted. He wanted to know how this all came about. So, we told him all the details.

Now, as I'm telling my part, the Spirit of God manifests again in the room, and the man's eyes were watering. I said, "The only reason I believe God got me involved is because I'm his preacher and I love to share the good news of Jesus, and I know this was an evil deed, but the other people, the family members, need to know, God sees, God hears, God knows, and He is in the redemption business." Detective Thomas was just astonished at what was happening in that little cubicle with only three chairs in it and these walls that were soundproof. He looked up at me, "Miss Kitty, now that I know that your heart is pure and your hands are clean, I'll tell you what we know. There was a prostitution/pornography ring; we believe it is connected with the boat God revealed to you ladies. I can't say all I know, but I can tell you that that ring was broken up to put a stop to these ungodly people. I will now follow up with Jim Marlin, the investigator for the water patrol and we are going to compare notes, and we are going to see where we take it from here."

So, Larry, Jim, and Doug confirmed everything with each other and the Father was gracious enough to let us breathe easy and let us sit back and wait until they did what they had to do. Then on a specific date, the Lord told me to go see the deputy sheriff who was in our county in Marshville, MO. He said, "I want you to go see him today, and don't make an appointment, go see him and tell him what I told you about this case." I knew the deputy because he was one of my regular customers who loved to come and eat at the restaurant. Come and get your buffalo burgers, fried chicken and biscuits, and gravy, etc.. He was just a really sweet Baptist brother. I called over there and said, "CE, I need to talk to you today. I need to come at 3:00. He said, "well, Kitty, I have a court case at 3:00, I won't even be in my office." I said, "Well, I'll go to your office and wait for you." He replied, "Ok Miss Kitty, I'll see you when I get out of court." I said, "I'll be in your office waiting." I had never been to his office before in my life.

So, I'm in his office at 3:00 p.m. (his case was a no-show), and he comes in and greets me. After a real sweet little sit-down time of fellowship, I began, "I have to tell you something that's happened and then some confirmations. As I told him, his eyes welled up with tears. I said, "CE, this kind of story will preach, and if you were ever called to preach, buddy, this will preach. You can share the good news of Jesus Christ and how wonderful He is to see and know and love people in spite of themselves. That's why He sent His son."

Deputy CE quietly replied, "I thought I was called to preach when I was a young man, but then I realized I wasn't." I said, "if you were ever called, you are called and CE this will preach. And furthermore, you are going to be the next Sheriff of this county, in Jesus Name."

I finished telling him the things that happened in this revelation of the three missing women. There was a snuff video, which is very sad, but it's where they recorded them on film, and they abuse them and then murder. CE interrupted me in mid-sentence, "stop right there. How in the world could you possibly know that?" I said, "Because the Spirit of God is all up in this and He's the revealer of truth. Nothing is hidden that won't be revealed; nothing is done in secret that won't be shouted from the rooftops." He said, "Kitty that is amazing, only just this morning at 9:00, I found out there was a snuff video associated with the murder of these three women." I said, "Well CE, that's all I came to tell you, that God's got your number and He said that you're going to be the next Sheriff so that you can relax in that." He goes, "Well, I hope you're right." Of course, he was voted in the next term.

The next thing that happens is we finally get to have a second meet and greet with the detective. He said, "All I can tell you is, everything you told us is accurate, and it has been confirmed over and over. The only problem we have is we haven't found circumstantial evidence to connect the criminals to the crime." I replied:

"Listen, that doesn't concern me. What concerns me is that God has a voice and He was heard. You said and saw the confirmations. I told him about CE, the deputy who became a Sheriff in my county." He said, "This is just amazing." He was a church member of that Cornerstone Church that I had been to and broke the curse of the vow of poverty over (covered in another chapter).

What is the take-away for you in all of this dear reader? That you might know and is be assured that there is the Spirit of God working, and then there is the power of God that comes along with hearing the Spirit of God. The demonstration of Spirit leads to the demonstration of power. God has done miracles, signs, and wonders, and I believe if you are a first partaker and you yield to Him and go to the secret place, there is nothing He won't tell you. There is absolutely nothing He won't tell you if He knows you're going to be faithful to obey Him and walk it out. How many people have begun and they get afraid? There is no place for fear. The fear of the Lord is clean, and every other fear is unclean. There was never any harm; there was never any downturn to this story. Waiting was the fun part. You know when you hear something like that, you think it's just going to be revealed overnight, but over time I was able to share this story with those, let us say who have ears to hear, and God told us to put this story in this book for this time.

Chapter Eleven

THE JERICHO DRIVE

Russ:

We could write a veritable encyclopedia of the things that God has done in our lives and the adventures we have experienced. The last thing we want to share in this book is about a nationwide assignment that laid the foundation for what Father's Heart Ministry would become in the early days of our work together.

Kitty and I came together to work in ministry in 2007 and married in 2010. During those years, we continued in the work-a-day world, although we had a keen desire to be full-time for the Lord. After marrying in October of that year, we set up house in Republic, Missouri. At the time we kept the business in Clinton Missouri going having hired an employee to take care of things part of the week, and we would then go up toward the end of the week for a few days. Denise Allsop, a good friend (who would eventually become one of the first employees of Father's Heart Ministry) had at first offered Kitty a job managing her speech pathology practice. This was a working arrangement, and we worked to remain faithful – all the while believing God that one day Father's Heart

Ministry would be our full-time employ.

One day, Kitty and I were discussing these things and looking forward to the year ahead wondering what would unfold for us in the coming months. Kitty asked the question, "Russ, what is your highest heart's desire?" It was difficult for me to answer. From my early twenties until God put me in the business world all I'd ever known was full-time ministry, first as the pastor of two churches over the course of 20 years and then working as the assistant overseer of a small denomination with its headquarters in Southeast Missouri. Kitty asked the question and wouldn't let me squirm out of answering. Finally, with tears in my eyes, I admitted that my greatest desire at that time was to work full-time dedicated to the Lord.

"That's it then," she declared. "Let's believe we receive and expect that being full-time in ministry is exactly what the Father has in store for us."

One thing you have to know is that prayer and faith believing are part of the equation of seeing a breakthrough from God, but it isn't the only thing. You must put legs to your prayers. A short time later, I was at my desk, and Kitty came in to make an announcement:

"God says that we are to take the vacation money we've been saving up and lay it at Prophet Kim Clement's feet."

Instantly, I knew that was God but stated one

observation at the same time. "If we do that fine, but there will be no vacation." It wasn't precisely a faith-filled declaration, but nonetheless, I sat down and wrote a letter in my own hand to send with the check we wanted Kim to receive. It was a large amount of money for us at the time, $1000.00. In my letter, we stated that this was our vacation money but that we would rather lay this at Kim's feet than go on vacation. This act of obedience would reap for us miraculous rewards. We asked Kim if he was so inclined, to pray for us because we were believing to be full time for the Lord and then we mailed the gift to his ministry address.

A few days later, our phone rang, and there was an excited friend on the other line. "It's you. It's you!" We weren't sure what she was talking about, but she went on to say that Kim Clement was reading letters on the air and mentioned a "Russ and Kitty" who had sacrificed to give their vacation money to the Lord. He went on to say that this Russ and Kitty didn't ask for a million dollars or anything for themselves but only to be full time in the ministry of the gospel. A day or so later, we received a beautiful drawing in the form of a note in Kim's own hand agreeing with us for our heart's desire.

Four months later, we stepped out of the employment we were in, sold the business, and we've been full-time in ministry from that day on. This was just the beginning of the adventures of Russ and Kitty. I thought there would be no vacation, but in fact, we were blessed to go on vacation, leaving Republic

Missouri and driving across Kansas to visit Royal Gorge, Colorado. This would be a big part of our story because coming back, driving across the plains, the Spirit of God descended into that car and began to speak with me. I was driving at the time, and Kitty was dozing in the passenger side. When she awoke, I shared with her the instructions God had given:

"We are supposed to give away all our possessions, get in our car, and drive across the country preaching the gospel."

Just saying the words made our ears ring, but we knew it was God. The Father had also said that after spending a year non-stop on the road, we would fly to Europe and preach the gospel in twelve countries before returning home again. All of this would come to pass, and God showed His power and displayed His glory in our lives and around the world. It took us a month to find ways to give away all our furniture and appliances. We sought out needy people and worthy ministries locally to us and asked them to come and take away all our personal property. We gave away all our things until there was nothing left except what we thought we would need to live life on the road. Even those few items we gave away in the first few months of what we called "The Jericho Drive" around the country. We figured if it didn't come into the hotel room at night, then we didn't need it and found Samaritan centers and benevolence ministries here and there to give 90% of what we'd packed in the car away as well.

When you start out obeying God, there are always surprises and not always pleasant ones. When we had packed and were pulling out of our apartment complex to make this grand journey – low and behold – someone rear-ended us damaging our car!

After extracting ourselves from that mess, we made our way east because that was where God told us the Jericho Drive would begin. In traveling to the east coast, we had not made any previous preparation for where we would be or what we would do. This was all by God's design. He had spoken to us that we would begin the Jericho Drive in Columbia, SC. One of our early supporters lived there – a chiropractor by the name of Vernishia Robinson. The Lord told us that we would stay for a time at Vernishia's home but that we couldn't call her ahead of time to make the arrangements or even see that it was possible. How would that possibly work out? By divine design of course. As we were driving down the highway, the cell phone rang and who might it be but Vernishia! She was bubbling over with excitement as she gave the reasons for her call:

"Papa Russ and Mama Kitty the Lord laid you on my heart, and I don't know where you are at or what you are doing, but you have to come and stay in my home! You have to stay in my guest room, and I have to cook for you and care for you by the leading of the Lord…"

When she finished speaking, it was her turn to be astonished to learn that God had already instructed us and we were on our way to her home after making a stop in Destin Florida to visit with Bill Lackie, the head of the Christian International Prophetic School. We made our way to the Emerald Coast of Florida and secured lodging on Scenic 30A just across the street from beach access. We contacted Prophet Bill and were thankful to find that he was available and agreed to see us. We visited in his office for about two hours, and during that time he prophesied to us that God would confirm the Jericho Drive by two things. A meteor would strike a city, and there would be an earthquake also – as a sign that we were hearing God correctly and that He was indeed with us on this coast to coast prophetic trek. That sounded fantastic and beyond plausibility to us, but at the same time, we understood the prophetic character of things in our life and tucked those things in our heart.

The very next day, an earthquake struck Seagrove Beach where we were staying. Kitty was downstairs in the condo laundry room, and I was upstairs doing prophetic counseling with a government contractor from the Philippines. Suddenly I heard a loud thud, and the entire building shook. My first thought was that a vehicle had struck the building, although our rented condo was far back from the street. Then another thud, this time much stronger shaking the structure even more. I stepped outside on the balcony and looked down toward the laundry where Kitty was. She also heard and felt the tremor and stepped outside, looking back up at me. The strange thing was that none of the other tenants came outside to investigate. Neither were there any car alarms going off as a result of the tremor and shaking. We couldn't explain it then or now, but the first sign Bill Lackie prophesied came to pass the very next day. The second sign would soon be revealed as well.

A few weeks later, we arrived in Columbia, SC, and stayed with Vernishia for a week or so. We held several prophetic meetings including meetings with "Vee" and her friends and family and also several meetings hosted by Bishop Nancy Drew of the Evangelical Protestant Church. God made Himself known in a profound way as secrets of men's hearts were revealed, and lives were changed by the prophetic word. Those relationships solidified during that visit and have lasted right down to the time of this writing.

The day came that we departed Columbia and headed toward Atlanta – our next stop. The drive was long, and we planned to stop over in Augusta for the night. We quickly arranged for a meeting room in a nearby restaurant and e-mailed an invitation to our friends and supporters to join us for an impromptu prophetic meeting. This was how it went during the entire Jericho Drive. We installed a live, real-time map on our website that showed our exact position to our visitors. It was an attention-getter and as they watched online as we traveled we would get an e-mail saying "you are five miles from my home – take Exit 5 and meet me at Denny's diner and I'll buy you lunch…" There was no plan, no advance person setting up meetings or marketing our ministry. God was orchestrating it all as we traveled to 66 cities that year and crossing the nation four times.

As we were on our way to Augusta, the news was reporting that a meteor had broken up over Chelyabinsk, Russia. We remembered the word of the Lord from Prophet Bill that there would be an earthquake and a meteor would strike a city. The Lord instructed me to look this up and research this city. What I found was astonishing. Chelyabinsk, Russia was, in fact, the SISTER CITY of Columbia, SC, where God told us to commence the Jericho Drive. Another powerful confirmation! Initially, when Bill said a meteor would strike a city, I thought "well Bill doesn't know his science. When a meteor enters the atmosphere, it is considered a meteorite and no longer a meteor. However, God and Bill got it right the first time because astrophysicists reported that this meteor was so giant that even after it entered the atmosphere, it was still considered a meteor! Go figure!

We traveled on toward Atlanta, holding a robust series of prophetic meetings there and then on to smaller cities such as Hattiesburg, MS where we met with a very small church meeting in a tiny room in a dilapidated building. The word of the Lord to this group was that they were going to grow rapidly and soon occupy a large building in a prime location in the city. In just a few months after our departure, New Hope New Life church moved into a 10,000 square foot building to accommodate their growing congregation that has been on the increase ever since!

After meetings in Birmingham and Nashville, we

were making our way toward Oklahoma City when a phone call came. At first, I thought it was a joke and hung up. Then an e-mail came with an explanation that the Travel Channel wanted Kitty and I to appear on one of their programs and talk about a series of teachings I had published online about the Spirit of Python. The Florida Everglades were and still are overrun by pythons, and a python spirit is a spirit of divination such as Paul dealt with in Philippi when he confronted the woman possessed with a spirit of divination. The inspiration for the teaching series was a leading news item showing a python wrapped around the jet engine pylon of a commercial carrier at 30,000 feet that was still alive when it landed. Kitty says anything that makes you do a double-take pray to interpret. This was the spirit of python in high places seeking to infest our country with the spirit of divination to bring our population into captivity to its influence.

We arrived in Oklahoma City and found airline tickets to West Palm Beach, awaiting us, and we flew down for the interview. They put us up in a hotel the night before, and a car came to collect us the next morning. They had rented a beautiful church with lovely stained-glass windows to film the interview. The film crew was Canadian by extraction, and the French-Canadian director sat down opposite me and began the discussion. You can still see this interview on re-runs on the Travel Channel under the heading of "Mysteries of National Parks." This was all very interesting, but the glory of God came forth after the cameras were turned off. I asked the director to please let me know if any part of the interview would actually be used in the series. He smiled and said, "I assure you that everything you shared will go into the program…"

He went on to explain that when he had gotten out of bed that morning, he'd had an excruciating migraine. He had suffered from this condition for all his life and more often than not would have to go to the ER to find some relief. He almost canceled our interview, but "something" urged him on. When he introduced himself to us, his headache was still raging – BUT – the moment he sat down to conduct the interview, the migraine instantly lifted, and he was totally well in that moment. Once again – God – as promised showed his power and displayed His glory in our lives as we chose to obey Him fully no matter what.

What is your take away from this story of the Jericho Drive? What is God telling you to do? What are you talking yourself out of in terms of sacrificial obedience? We started out on the Jericho Drive by giving up our home and giving all of our personal possessions away. We went on the road for a solid year with no planning and no promise of provision. In the end, what I thought would be a financial strain turned out to be a financial windfall. We not only made our expenses but returned home to Branson, Missouri with tens of thousands of dollars in the black and God had more than taken care of us on our big adventure.

Are you willing to adventure for God? Then listen to

His voice and do what He says. Refuse to be talked out of it by friends, family, or your own common sense. God's way of looking at things doesn't always make sense but if you listen and obey you will do exploits in His name and come out on the other side with your testimony intact, shouting victory because you made it through!